D0495906

party food

Produced by **ACP**books

Printed by Bookbuilders, China.
Published by ACP Publishing Pty Limited, 54 Park Street, Sydney, NSW 2000 (GPO Box 4088, Sydney, NSW 2001),
phone (02) 9282 8618, fax (02) 9267 9438, acpbooks@acp.com.au www.acpbooks.com.au
AUSTRALIA: Distributed by Network Services, GPO Box 4088, Sydney, NSW 2001, phone (02) 9282 8777, fax (02) 9264 3278.
UNITED KINGDOM: Distributed by Australian Consolidated Press (UK), Moulton Park Business Centre, Red House Road,
Moulton Park, Northampton, NN3 6AQ, phone (01604) 497 531, fax (01604) 497 533, acpukltd@aol.com
CANADA: Distributed by Whitecap Books Ltd, 351 Lynn Avenue, North Vancouver, BC, V7J 2C4,
phone (604) 980 9852, fax (604) 980 8197, customerservice@whitecap.ca www.whitecap.ca
NEW ZEALAND: Distributed by Netlink Distribution Company, ACP Media Centre, Cnr Fanshawe and Beaumont Streets,
Westhaven, Auckland (PO Box 47906, Ponsonby, Auckland, NZ), phone (9) 366 9966, ask@ndcnz.co.nz

Gourmet party food.
Includes index.
ISBN 1 86396 288 3.
1. Cookery. 2. Entertaining. I. Australian Gourmet Traveller.
641.568
© ACP Publishing Pty Limited 2003
ABN 18 053 273 546
This publication is copyright. No part of it may be reproduced or transmitted in any form
without the written permission of the publishers. First published in 2003.
Front cover: Saffron roulade with lemon crème fraîche and salmon roe, page 16. Back cover: Betel leaves topped with prawns and galangal, page 20.

AUSTRALIAN GOURMET TRAVELLER
Editor Judy Sarris
Food editor Leanne Kitchen
Deputy food editor Sophia Young
Assistant food editors Christine Osmond, Kathleen Gandy

ACP BOOKS
Editorial director Susan Tomnay
Creative director Hieu Chi Nguyen
Senior editor Lynda Wilton
Publishing manager (sales) Brian Cearnes
Publishing manager (rights & new projects) Jane Hazell
Brand manager Donna Gianniotis
Production manager Carol Currie
Business manager Sally Lees
Assistant business analyst Martin Howes
Studio manager Caryl Wiggins
Pre-press Harry Palmer
Editorial & sales coordinator Caroline Lowry
Editorial assistant Karen Lai

Photographer Chris Chen
Stylist Kristen Anderson
Recipes by Allan Campion, Bronwen Clark, Rodney Dunn,
Kathleen Gandy, Fiona Hammond, Jane Hann,
Leanne Kitchen, Lynne Mullins, Christine Osmond,
Louise Pickford, Susie Smith, Kathy Snowball, Sophia Young
Food preparation by Rodney Dunn
Cover styled by Eric Matthews

Chief executive officer John Alexander
Group publisher Jill Baker
Publisher Sue Wannan

THANKS TO THESE STOCKISTS AND SUPPLIERS
Accoutrement phone (02) 9969 1031 or (02) 9418 2992
All Hand Made phone (02) 9386 4099
Arte Flowers Sydney phone (02) 9328 0402
Atmosphere phone (02) 8354 1571
Bison Homewares phone (02) 6284 2334
Boxx phone (02) 9280 1878
Camargue phone (02) 9960 6234
Country Road HomeWear phone 1800 801 911
Design Mode International phone (02) 9998 8200
The Essential Ingredient phone (02) 9550 5477
Funkis Swedish Forms (head office) phone (02) 9130 6445
FY2K phone (02) 9281 1771
Hermès phone (02) 9223 4007
Malcolm Greenwood phone (02) 9953 8613
Mud Australia phone (02) 9518 0220
Orrefors Kosta Boda (head office) phone (02) 9913 4200
Orson & Blake phone (02) 9326 1155
Roylston House phone (02) 9331 3033
Spence & Lyda phone (02) 9212 6747

AUSTRALIAN GOURMET TRAVELLER

party food

ACPbooks

contents

party planning guide

A key element of party planning is to ensure there is sufficient and appropriate food. The recipes in this book cover four broad situations: an elegant cocktail party, casual finger food, outdoor entertaining and catering for a crowd. Entertaining etiquette has relaxed somewhat over recent years, allowing hosts more flexibility in setting their own rules. It is not uncommon now, for example, for weddings to be celebrated outdoors with barefoot brides, or for a housewarming to be an excuse for a stylish cocktail party.

Decisions, decisions

Before you begin, it is important to make the following decisions:

What kind of party do you wish to give? Will it be a formal, elegant event or a casual, relaxed affair? Would you prefer to provide a meal (a sit-down dinner or informal buffet), or to serve a selection of canapés with drinks?

Wherever possible, choose a setting that complements the mood of the party: for instance, a garden suits a summery outdoor event or casual buffet, while an elegant cocktail party requires a room spacious enough for people to serve the food and for guests to circulate.

The time of day and duration of the event will determine what and how much food and drink should be provided. If the event is held around a mealtime, guests will expect to be offered the corresponding meal.

Getting organised

Once the menu has been chosen, make a comprehensive food shopping list, broken down into what can be purchased in advance and what needs to be purchased on the day. A corresponding list of both cooking and serving equipment and any storage needs you might have will help you determine whether the menu is overly ambitious. Do you have sufficient oven trays, crockery, cutlery, serving platters, trays, glasses and refrigerator space? A list outlining a food preparation plan is extremely useful, breaking down the time needed to prepare and cook the chosen dishes.

Time savers

Base menus around dishes which only require plating, reheating or quick assembly before serving, to minimise last-minute preparation.

For a stand-up and mingle occasion, if there are no bar staff, set up tables of food and drink for people to help themselves.

Choose some dishes that can be set out just before guests are expected and which only need to be replenished: for example, a range of olives, artisanal cheeses and interesting breads. Determine if any components can be prepared in advance. Check the index on page 126 to find out which of our recipes can be completely prepared in advance.

Take a creative look at equipment you already have, such as bread boards (which can double as platters), vases and bowls, to find inspiration for table-setting and presentation.

Choosing food

The menu should reflect a balance of flavours and textures (ie, a mix of meat, poultry, seafood, vegetable-based, substantial and light, and savoury and sweet dishes). Dietary considerations of guests, such as food allergies, religious observances and preferences, should also be taken into account. Basing a menu around seasonal ingredients means that not only will the food be at its best, but also readily available and reasonably priced. Always bear in mind such practicalities as refrigerator space and oven and stove-top capacity.

Stress can be minimised if menu planning takes into account the cooking time of dishes which are to be served simultaneously. Serve hot and room-temperature or cold dishes together for guests to help themselves, where appropriate. For informal entertaining, barbecues are ideal, as accompanying dishes can be prepared in advance to serve at room temperature, and marinated seafood, meat or poultry can be quickly barbecued close to serving. Timing can be more critical for winter entertaining, as people tend to prefer hot dishes, so it is a good idea to prepare a few choices which only require last-minute reheating or baking. Minimise the number of recipes that require a lot of attention in the kitchen after your guests have arrived.

Offer contrasting dishes: for example, avoid canapés that are all bread- or pastry-based, or a buffet of all rich, creamy dishes. Similarly, offer dishes with a range of colours and shapes: for instance, avoid serving all-round canapés at a cocktail party or all-red vegetable side dishes when cooking for a crowd.

As a rough guide, when choosing canapés, you should allow:
- 4-5 pieces per person for pre-dinner nibbles;
- 4-5 pieces per person for the first hour and 4 pieces for each hour after that for a cocktail party;
- 12-14 pieces per person for an entire afternoon or evening.

Checklist

- Guest list, invitations and RSVPs
- Menu and complete shopping list, including days in advance items can be purchased
- Food preparation list
- Equipment list, covering the preparation and serving of food
- Table and room decorations
- Garbage bags/bins
- Seating
- Music
- Indoor alternative for outdoor parties in case of inclement weather
- Plenty of ice; it is easy to underestimate the amount needed for any party

Fennel seed allumettes

125g plain flour
90g cold unsalted butter, chopped
3 teaspoons fennel seeds
50g finely grated parmesan
50g finely grated cheddar
2 egg yolks
Flaked sea salt, for sprinkling

Process flour, butter, fennel seeds, cheeses, 1 egg yolk and a pinch of sea salt in a food processor until mixture just comes together. Transfer dough to a lightly floured surface, knead briefly until smooth, then shape into a flat rectangle, wrap in plastic wrap and refrigerate for 1 hour.

Roll out pastry on a lightly floured surface to a 20x30cm rectangle, then, using a large sharp knife, trim edges and cut pastry widthways into 5mm-thick strips, then carefully transfer to baking paper-lined oven trays. Combine remaining egg yolk with 1 teaspoon water, brush strips with egg mixture and sprinkle lightly with flaked sea salt.

Bake at 180C for 15 minutes or until golden.

Cool on oven trays for 5 minutes, then transfer to a wire rack to cool completely.

Fennel seed allumettes will keep in an airtight container for up to 1 week.

Makes about 30

Crab bisque

4 live blue swimmer crabs (see note)
100ml olive oil
1 onion, chopped
1 carrot, chopped
1 stalk of celery, chopped
1 leek, white part only, chopped
1 clove of garlic, chopped
250ml dry white wine
1.25 litres fish stock
1 fresh bay leaf
4 sprigs of thyme
2 tomatoes, chopped
1 tablespoon tomato paste
50g (¼ cup) long grain rice
2 tablespoons brandy
300ml pouring cream
Snowpea shoots, leaves only, or
    watercress leaves, to serve

Using a cleaver or large heavy knife, chop crabs into quarters and crack claws.

Heat oil in a large heavy-based saucepan, add onion, carrot, celery, leek and garlic and cook over high heat, stirring frequently, for 10-12 minutes or until lightly browned. Add crab pieces and cook for another 5-6 minutes or until crabs have changed colour. Add remaining ingredients except for brandy and cream, season to taste with sea salt and freshly ground black pepper, bring to the boil, then reduce heat to low and simmer for 45 minutes.

Strain mixture into a bowl, reserving liquid, remove and discard large pieces of shell and claws, extracting as much meat as possible, then return solids to same pan and, using a heavy rolling pin or mallet, crush remaining small pieces of shell as finely as possible. Process crushed shells and solids in a food processor, in batches, with ½ cup reserved liquid at a time until coarsely crushed, strain mixture through a mouli or potato ricer, then strain again through a fine sieve into a saucepan. Add brandy and bring to the boil. Reduce heat, add cream and bring bisque to just below boiling point, then season to taste.

At this stage of preparation, bisque will keep refrigerated for up to 3 days.

Using a blender, froth hot bisque, in batches, then pour into twenty-five 60ml cups or glasses, top with a few picked leaves of snowpea shoots, if using, and serve immediately.

Makes about 1.5 litres
Notes: Place the crabs in the freezer for 30 minutes, to humanely put them to sleep, before preparing them for cooking. For entrée size, serves 6-8 people.

Steak tartare and anchoïade toasts

It is best to combine all the ingredients for this recipe just before serving, as the minced beef fillet will discolour quickly.

1 thin sourdough baguette, cut into 6mm-thick slices
Olive oil
420g piece of beef fillet
2 tablespoons finely chopped shallots
2 tablespoons finely chopped cornichons
1 tablespoon baby capers, rinsed and finely chopped
2 tablespoons finely chopped flat-leaf parsley
2 teaspoons Dijon mustard
2 teaspoons Worcestershire sauce
2 egg yolks
Tabasco, to taste
Finely chopped chives, to serve
Anchoïade
60g drained anchovy fillets
1 clove of garlic, finely chopped
1 egg yolk
½ cup olive oil
Lemon juice, to taste

Lightly brush bread slices with olive oil, then place on an oven tray and bake at 180C for 15 minutes or until crisp and golden.

For anchoïade, place anchovies and garlic in a mortar and pound with a pestle until smooth. Transfer mixture to a small bowl, then stir in egg yolk. Whisking continuously, add oil in a thin, steady stream until well combined, then stir in lemon juice to taste. Cover and refrigerate until required.

Using an electric or hand-operated mincer, mince beef, then combine in a bowl with remaining ingredients and season to taste with sea salt and freshly ground black pepper.

Top each croûton with ½ teaspoon anchoïade, then top with 2 heaped teaspoons steak tartare, drizzle with a little olive oil and sprinkle with chives.
Makes about 45

Tomato confit, olive and anchovy tarts

1 tablespoon olive oil

1 onion, thinly sliced

1 clove of garlic, finely chopped

6 anchovy fillets, chopped

1 teaspoon thyme leaves

185g (1 cup) niçoise or other small black olives, pitted

Pastry

180g cold butter, chopped

240g plain flour

Tomato confit

200g grape tomatoes or small cherry tomatoes

⅓ cup extra virgin olive oil

2 cloves of garlic, unpeeled

3 sprigs of thyme

For pastry, process butter, flour and a pinch of salt in a food processor until mixture resembles breadcrumbs, then add ¼ cup iced water and process until mixture just comes together. Form dough into a disc, then wrap in plastic wrap and refrigerate for 1 hour.

Roll out half the pastry on a lightly floured surface until 2-3mm thick, then, using a 3.5x8cm boat-shaped tart tin as a guide, cut boat shapes from pastry and transfer to a baking paper-lined tray, reserving pastry scraps. Repeat with remaining pastry and combined pastry scraps. Line twelve 3.5x8cm boat-shaped tart tins with pastry shapes, then cover tart shells and pastry shapes with plastic wrap and refrigerate for one hour. Line tart shells with baking paper, then fill with dried rice or beans and bake at 200C for 7 minutes. Remove paper and beans and bake for another 5-7 minutes or until dry and golden, then cool. Repeat with remaining pastry shapes and tart tins.

For tomato confit, place tomatoes in a single layer in an ovenproof dish, add remaining ingredients, season to taste with sea salt and freshly ground black pepper and combine well. Bake at 140C for 25-30 minutes or until tomatoes are just soft but skins have not split, then remove from oven and stand until required.

Meanwhile, heat olive oil in a small heavy-based saucepan, add onion, garlic and a pinch of sea salt and cook, partially covered, stirring frequently, over low heat for 15-20 minutes or until soft and lightly caramelised. Add anchovies and thyme and cook for another 2-3 minutes or until well combined. Using a blender, process onion mixture until smooth.

Place olives in a bowl and combine with 1 tablespoon tomato confit cooking juices.

To assemble, spoon 1 scant teaspoon onion mixture into each tart shell, then top with 1 drained confit tomato and 3 olives.

Tarts can be served immediately at room temperature, or warm. To serve warm, place filled tarts on an oven tray and cook at 180C for 8-10 minutes.

Makes about 42

Saffron roulade with lemon crème fraîche and salmon roe

200g crème fraîche
1 teaspoon finely grated lemon rind
100g salmon roe
Small sprigs of dill, optional, to serve
Saffron roulade
1 cup milk
Pinch of saffron threads
40g butter
35g (¼ cup) plain flour
3 eggs, separated

For saffron roulade, place milk and saffron in a small saucepan and heat until just warm. Remove from heat and stand for 20 minutes, then strain through a fine sieve.

Melt butter in a small saucepan, add flour and combine well, then cook over low heat, stirring continuously, for 1-2 minutes or until mixture just starts to change colour. Whisking continuously, gradually add milk mixture, then simmer, stirring frequently, for 2 minutes or until mixture has thickened. Remove from heat, cool a little, then stir in egg yolks, one at a time, beating well after each. Season to taste with sea salt, transfer mixture to a bowl and cover closely with plastic wrap, then cool to room temperature.

Using an electric mixer, whisk egg whites until stiff peaks form, then, using a large metal spoon, fold egg whites into saffron mixture in two batches. Pour mixture into a baking paper-lined 25x38cm shallow oven tray, smooth top and bake at 200C for 15 minutes or until just set and barely coloured. Turn out roulade onto a clean tea towel, peel off baking paper, cut roulade in half widthways and trim long sides. While still warm, carefully roll up each half from a long side, then cool, seam-side down.

Place crème fraîche and lemon rind in a bowl, season to taste, then, using a wooden spoon, beat until smooth. Reserve ¼ cup mixture, cover and refrigerate until required. Transfer each roulade to a large piece of plastic wrap and carefully unroll. Spread remaining crème fraîche mixture over roulades, leaving a 1cm border. Using the plastic wrap as a guide, roll up roulades firmly and twist ends to seal, then refrigerate for 1 hour. Unsliced roulade will keep refrigerated for up to 3 days.

To serve, unwrap roulade, then cut into 2cm-thick rounds. Top each round with a little reserved crème fraîche, then spoon ½ teaspoon salmon roe over each and top with dill sprigs, if using.

Makes about 30 slices

Leek terrine with goat's curd

Assemble these canapés just before serving, or toasts may become soggy.

2.2kg small leeks
2 cups chicken stock
125ml dry white wine
50g butter
2 sprigs of thyme
1 fresh bay leaf
2 cloves of garlic
1 loaf of brioche or sourdough, crusts removed
　and cut into 1cm-thick slices
175g goat's curd
Chervil sprigs and extra virgin olive oil, to serve

Reserve 2 leeks, then trim green tops from remaining leeks and remove tough outer leaves. Rinse well, then place in a wide heavy-based saucepan with stock, wine, butter, thyme, bay leaf and garlic and season to taste with sea salt and freshly ground black pepper. Cover closely with a circle of buttered baking paper, then simmer gently for 15-20 minutes or until very tender. Drain leeks and transfer to a colander to cool. Running your hands down the leeks, squeeze out as much excess liquid as possible.

Meanwhile, cut reserved leeks in half lengthways, separate layers and rinse well, then blanch in boiling salted water for 1 minute or until just tender. Drain and refresh in iced water, then pat dry with absorbent paper.

Line a 4x30cm 5.5cm-deep terrine mould with plastic wrap and place blanched leek strips widthways in slightly overlapping layers to completely line mould (leek strips will overhang sides of terrine). Season braised leeks to taste, then place lengthways into terrine, trimming where necessary so leeks fit snugly (leeks may not come all the way to top of terrine). Press down firmly, then fold over leek strips to cover top of terrine, trimming excess. Cover with plastic wrap and weight with small food cans, then refrigerate overnight.

Unmould terrine and cut off a 1cm-thick slice. Using slice as a guide, cut brioche into squares and place on an oven tray, then bake at 180C for 10 minutes or until golden. Transfer toasts to wire racks and cool.

To assemble, spread each toast with a little goat's curd, then cut remaining terrine into 1cm-thick slices and place on toasts. Top each with ½ teaspoon curd and a small sprig of chervil, then drizzle with olive oil and season to taste with a little freshly ground black pepper. **Makes about 30 pieces**

Betel leaves topped with prawns and galangal

2 tablespoons peanut oil

2 cloves of garlic, crushed

1 fresh long red chilli, seeded and finely chopped

6cm piece of ginger, peeled and finely grated

6cm piece of galangal, peeled and finely grated

1.2kg medium green prawns, peeled,
    cleaned and coarsely chopped

1½ tablespoons fish sauce

1 tablespoon coconut cream

250g beansprouts

1 cup coriander leaves

20 betel leaves, washed and dried

35g (¼ cup) raw peanuts, roasted
    and coarsely chopped

Lime wedges, optional, to serve

Heat a wok or large frying pan over high heat. Add oil and heat until oil just begins to smoke, then add half the garlic, chilli, ginger and galangal and stir-fry for 30 seconds. Add half the prawns and stir-fry for 3 minutes. Add half the fish sauce and coconut cream, toss to combine, then remove from heat and transfer to a large bowl. Repeat with remaining halves of same ingredients, then add to prawn mixture in bowl and cool for 10 minutes. Stir in beansprouts and coriander leaves. Top betel leaves with 2 tablespoon prawn mixture, then sprinkle with peanuts and serve with lime wedges, if using.

Makes 20

Little pancakes with avruga

Alternative toppings could include salmon roe, smoked salmon, smoked trout or smoked chicken.

20g butter, chopped
200g crème fraîche
1 onion, finely chopped
5 hard-boiled eggs, yolks and whites
   finely chopped separately
2 120g jars avruga

Pancakes
2 eggs, at room temperature
1 tablespoon melted butter, cooled
150g plain wholemeal flour
1 teaspoon baking powder
1 teaspoon caster sugar
¾ cup lukewarm milk

For pancakes, whisk together eggs and melted butter until just combined. In another bowl, combine flour, baking powder, sugar and ¼ teaspoon salt, fold in egg mixture and milk and stir until smooth.

Melt a little butter in a heavy-based frying pan, then cook heaped teaspoonfuls of batter, in batches, for 1-2 minutes on each side or until golden, adding more butter as necessary. Transfer to a baking paper-covered wire rack to cool. Serve pancakes topped with crème fraîche, onion, hard-boiled egg yolk, egg white and avruga.
Makes 40-45

Scallops with mint and ginger salad

If scallops on the half shell are unavailable, try serving the salad and scallops on small Chinese soup spoons instead.

100ml extra virgin olive oil
1 tablespoon lime juice
1 teaspoon finely grated ginger
1½ cup small mint leaves
2 large lebanese cucumbers, peeled, halved
    lengthwise, seeded and very thinly sliced
24 scallop on the half shell
Small wooden cocktail forks, to serve

Place 60ml olive oil, lime juice, ginger and sea salt to taste in a bowl and whisk until well combined. Add mint leaves and cucumber and toss to coat.

Remove scallops from shells, place in a bowl, drizzle with remaining olive oil and toss gently to coat. Rinse and dry scallop shells and place on a large platter, then spoon a little salad mixture onto each shell. Char-grill scallops over high heat for 30 seconds on each side or until just tender, then top each salad with a scallop and serve immediately with small wooden cocktail forks.
Makes 24

Corn cakes with Japanese chicken

3 cobs of corn, husks and silks removed
Olive oil
5 green onions, thinly sliced
2 chicken breast fillets (200g each)
2 lebanese cucumbers, finely chopped
35g (¼ cup) self-raising flour
½ teaspoon bicarbonate of soda
3 eggs, lightly beaten
90g pickled ginger, drained
Wasabi mayonnaise
2 egg yolks
1 tablespoon rice vinegar
1 cup vegetable oil
3 teaspoons wasabi paste

Using a sharp knife, cut kernels from corn cobs. Heat 1 teaspoon olive oil in a large non-stick frying pan, add corn and stir over medium heat for 6-8 minutes or until soft. Stir in green onion and cook for another minute, then remove from pan.

Steam chicken breasts, covered, in a steamer over a saucepan of simmering water, for 12-15 minutes or until cooked through. Cool, then tear chicken into fine shreds and combine in a bowl with cucumber.

For wasabi mayonnaise, process egg yolks and rice vinegar in a food processor until well combined, then, with the motor running, gradually add oil drop by drop at first, then in a steady stream, until mixture is thick and well combined. Transfer mayonnaise to a bowl, stir in wasabi paste, then season to taste with sea salt and freshly ground black pepper.

Add mayonnaise to chicken mixture and mix well, then cover and refrigerate until required.

Place corn mixture in a bowl, sift over flour and bicarbonate of soda and mix well, then stir in beaten eggs and season to taste. Heat ½ tablespoon olive oil in a frying pan and cook tablespoons of mixture, 4 at a time, over medium heat for 2 minutes on each side or until golden and cooked through, then transfer to a warm plate, cover and set aside. Repeat with remaining mixture. Serve corn cakes topped with chicken mixture and a piece of pickled ginger.
Makes about 30

Ribbon sandwiches

Salmon and lemon caper mayonnaise sandwiches

¾ cup mayonnaise
1 tablespoon salted capers, rinsed,
   drained and finely chopped
1 teaspoon Dijon mustard
1 tablespoon lemon juice
16 thin slices rye bread
8 slices smoked salmon (about 200g)
⅔ cup chervil sprigs (firmly packed)

Combine mayonnaise, capers, mustard and lemon juice in a bowl, then season to taste with freshly ground black pepper. Spread bread slices with lemon caper mayonnaise, then place salmon slices over half the bread slices, trimming as necessary. Scatter with chervil sprigs, then cover with remaining bread slices and, using a serrated hand or electric knife, trim crusts and cut each sandwich into three fingers. Cover with a damp tea towel until ready to serve.
Makes 24 sandwiches

Mushroom, cream cheese and prosciutto sandwiches

30g unsalted butter
200g fresh shiitake mushrooms, stalks removed,
   caps thinly sliced
200g swiss brown mushrooms, thinly sliced
1 tablespoon dry sherry or Madeira
24 thin slices (about 360g) prosciutto
150g cream cheese
2 tablespoons chopped flat-leaf parsley
16 thin slices white bread

Melt butter in a large frying pan, add mushrooms and cook over medium heat for 8-10 minutes or until soft and liquid has evaporated. Add sherry, combine well, then remove from heat and cool.

Heat a cast iron grill pan over medium heat and cook prosciutto, in batches, for 30-40 seconds on each side; prosciutto will shrink and darken in colour but not crisp. Drain on absorbent paper.

Process cream cheese, parsley and cooled mushrooms in a food processor until finely chopped and well combined. Season to taste with sea salt and freshly ground black pepper, then spread bread slices with cream cheese mixture. Place three pieces of prosciutto on half the bread slices, then cover with remaining bread. Using a hand or electric serrated knife, trim crusts and cut each sandwich into three fingers, then cover with a damp tea towel until ready to serve.
Makes 24 sandwiches

Little lamingtons

125g soft butter, plus extra,
  for greasing
165g (¾ cup) caster sugar
½ teaspoon vanilla extract
2 eggs
185g (1¼ cups) plain flour
2½ teaspoons baking powder
¼ cup milk
250g flaked coconut,
  crushed slightly

Icing

500g (3¼ cups) icing sugar, sifted
50g Dutch-process cocoa
40g soft butter
½ teaspoon vanilla extract
1 tablespoon cognac

Using an electric mixer, beat butter, sugar and vanilla until light and creamy. Add eggs one at a time, beating well after each. Stir in combined sifted flour and baking powder alternately with milk, in 2 batches, and stir until smooth. Spoon mixture into a greased and base-lined square 23cm cake tin and bake at 190C for 25-30 minutes or until a cake tester withdraws clean. Stand in tin for 10 minutes before turning out onto a wire rack to cool. Wrap in plastic wrap and store for 1 day for easier cutting.

For icing, combine all ingredients with 120ml boiling water in a heatproof bowl and stir until smooth.

Cut cake into 4cm squares and dip each one briefly into icing, then into coconut. Place lamingtons on a wire rack for 1-2 hours or until dry. Will keep in an airtight container for 4-5 days.

Makes about 25

Miniature tarts with lime curd, mango and raspberries

225g (1½ cups) plain flour

2 tablespoons icing sugar, plus extra, for dusting

2 tablespoons dessicated coconut

85g cold unsalted butter, chopped

1 egg, lightly beaten

1 mango, thinly sliced with a vegetable peeler

120g raspberries

Lime curd

4 egg yolks

110g (½ cup) caster sugar

1 tablespoon grated lime rind

½ cup lime juice

180g cold unsalted butter, chopped

For lime curd, whisk egg yolks, sugar and lime rind in a heatproof bowl over a saucepan of simmering water until sugar dissolves and mixture is pale, then stir in lime juice and mix well. Gradually add butter, piece by piece, stirring continuously until each piece has melted. Continue to stir until mixture thickens enough to coat the back of a wooden spoon. Do not boil. Cool to room temperature, then place in a sterilised jar. Lime curd will keep refrigerated for up to 2 weeks.

Process flour, icing sugar, coconut and butter in a food processor until mixture resembles breadcrumbs. Add egg and process until mixture just comes together.

Turn out on a lightly floured surface, knead until smooth, then form into a disc, wrap in plastic wrap and refrigerate for 30 minutes. Cut dough in half and roll out between 2 sheets of baking paper until 3mm thick. Using a 5cm pastry cutter, cut out rounds. Place rounds in 4cm tart tins, prick bases with a fork and bake at 180C for 10-12 minutes or until golden. Cool, then remove from tins.

Place a spoonful of curd in each tart shell, top with 1 slice of mango and a raspberry, then dust with extra icing sugar.

Makes 32 tarts

Profiteroles with orange cream and white chocolate

100g unsalted butter, chopped
2 teaspoons caster sugar
150g (1 cup) plain flour, sifted
5 eggs
120g white couverture chocolate,
   finely chopped
Orange cream
1 cup milk
200ml double cream
4 2cm strips of orange rind
4 egg yolks
55g (¼ cup) caster sugar
2 tablespoons plain flour
½ teaspoon vanilla extract

For orange cream, combine milk, cream and orange rind in a saucepan and bring just to the boil. Remove from heat and stand for 10 minutes to allow flavours to infuse.

Using an electric mixer, whisk egg yolks and sugar until thick and pale, then stir in flour and combine well. Remove orange rind from cream mixture, return mixture to the heat and bring to a simmer. Whisking continuously, pour a little hot cream mixture onto egg mixture, then add egg mixture to cream in pan. Whisk continuously over low-medium heat until mixture boils and thickens, then remove from heat and stir in vanilla. Transfer orange cream to a bowl, cover closely with plastic wrap, cool, then refrigerate until cold. Orange cream will keep refrigerated for up to 3 days.

Combine butter, sugar and 1 cup cold water in a saucepan and bring to the boil. Remove from heat, add flour all at once and, using a wooden spoon, stir vigorously, then return mixture to a low heat and stir for 1-2 minutes or until mixture comes away from side of pan. Immediately transfer mixture to the bowl of an electric mixer and, with motor running, add 4 eggs, one at a time, beating well after each. Spoon mixture into a piping bag fitted with a 2.5cm plain nozzle and pipe 3-4cm rounds, 5cm apart onto baking paper-lined oven trays. Lightly beat remaining egg with 1 teaspoon water, then brush rounds lightly with egg mixture and bake at 200C for 20 minutes or until crisp and golden. Transfer profiteroles to a wire rack, and, using a skewer or small knife, pierce a hole in the base of each profiterole, to allow steam to escape. Cool.

Cut profiteroles nearly in half widthways, leaving one side intact, then, using a teaspoon or piping bag fitted with a 2cm plain nozzle, fill centres with orange cream.

Melt chocolate in a bowl over a saucepan of simmering water, then, working quickly, use a dry warm spoon to drizzle melted chocolate over profiteroles.

Makes about 30
Note: Fill pastries with cream no more than 1 hour before serving. They are best eaten within 1 hour of filling.

Peking duck cones

1 Chinese barbecue duck
8 green onions
15 Peking duck pancakes, warmed
150g hoisin sauce
125g mustard cress (about 5 25g punnets)

Using a sharp knife, remove meat with skin from duck
in large pieces, then cut into thin strips. Cut each green
onion into 5cm lengths, then lengthways into thin strips.
    Cut each warmed pancake in half, place a piece of duck
in the centre at a 90 degree angle to the pancake's
straight side, spoon on a little hoisin sauce and top with
a few strips of green onion and mustard cress. Roll the
pancake into a cone shape, then place on a platter,
join-side down.
Makes about 30

Caramelised-onion and goat's-cheese pizza with rosemary oil

50g butter, chopped
3 large spanish onions, thinly sliced
120g goat's cheese, crumbled
1 tablespoon small rosemary sprigs
Rosemary oil
½ cup olive oil
4 small sprigs of rosemary, bruised
2 cloves of garlic, halved
Dough
1½ teaspoons dry yeast
Pinch of sugar
300g (2 cups) plain flour

For rosemary oil, combine all ingredients in a small saucepan and cook over medium heat until sizzling. Remove from heat, cover and stand for several hours or overnight. Strain.

Combine yeast, sugar, 30g flour and ¼ cup lukewarm water in a small bowl, cover and stand in a warm place for 10-15 minutes until foamy.

Process remaining flour, ¾ teaspoon salt, ¼ cup rosemary oil, yeast mixture and ¾ cup lukewarm water in a food processor until mixture forms a ball, then process for another minute. Place dough in a lightly oiled bowl, turn to coat with oil, then cover and leave in a draught-free place for 1-1½ hours or until doubled in size.

Meanwhile, heat butter in a large non-stick frying pan, add onion and cook over low-medium heat, stirring regularly, for 45 minutes or until very soft. Season to taste with sea salt and freshly ground black pepper. Cool.

Knock down dough and turn out onto a lightly floured surface. Knead briefly, roll out until 5mm-thick and line a greased, 23x30cm shallow metal oven tray. Trim excess dough, then spread caramelised onion over, top with crumbled goat's cheese, drizzle with remaining rosemary oil and scatter with rosemary sprigs. Bake pizza at 225C fan-forced setting (or 245C in a conventional oven) for 15 minutes. Carefully slide pizza off oven tray onto an oven rack and return to oven for another 3-4 minutes, or until dough is golden and base is crisp.

Cut lengthways into 5 strips, then cut each strip in half.
Makes 10 pieces

Warm brandade with walnut toasts

1 spunta potato (about 100g)
700g dried salt cod, soaked in
   cold water for 24 hours,
   changing the water 3 times
1 cup milk
100ml extra virgin olive oil
½ cup double cream
2 cloves of garlic, finely chopped
¼ teaspoon freshly grated nutmeg
2 loaves of walnut bread, cut into
   8mm-thick slices, lightly brushed
   with olive oil and char-grilled

Cook potato in boiling salted water until tender, then drain. When cool enough to handle, peel potato and mash coarsely.

Drain salt cod, then place in a saucepan with milk and just enough water to cover. Simmer for 10 minutes or until flesh flakes easily. Drain, then, when cool enough to handle, discard skin and bones and flake fish.

Combine oil and cream in a small saucepan and bring to just below the boil.

Combine potato, fish and garlic in a heavy-based saucepan and cook, using a simmer mat, over very low heat, stirring frequently with a wooden spoon until just warm. Stirring continuously, slowly add warm cream mixture to fish mixture and stir until smooth and well combined. Stir in nutmeg and season to taste with freshly ground black pepper.

Transfer brandade to a warm bowl and serve with char-grilled walnut bread.

Makes about 3 cups

Fig and fennel scones with washed-rind cheese

250g (1⅔ cups) self-raising flour
40g cold butter, chopped, plus extra,
    for greasing
60g (⅓ cup) chopped ready-soaked figs,
    stems removed
¼ teaspoon fennel seeds
150ml buttermilk
1 egg, lightly beaten with
    1 tablespoon water
Washed-rind cheese, to serve

Sift flour and a pinch of salt into a bowl and rub in butter until mixture resembles breadcrumbs.
Stir in figs and fennel seeds until combined, then, using a round-ended knife, stir in buttermilk and mix until dough just comes together. Knead gently on a lightly floured surface.

Press dough out on a lightly floured surface until 2.5cm-thick and, using a 4cm pastry cutter, cut out rounds. Place rounds 3cm apart on lightly greased oven trays, brush tops with egg mixture and bake at 220C for 12-15 minutes or until risen and golden.

Serve warm scones split and topped with cheese. Best made on day of serving.

Makes about 18

Broad bean dip with wilted chicory, roasted onions and accompaniments

200g (1⅓ cups) dried broad beans,
    soaked in water overnight, then drained
150g sebago potato (about 1 small potato),
    peeled and chopped
1 onion, chopped
1 stalk of celery
1 dried bay leaf
¼ cup extra virgin olive oil
2 tablespoons lemon juice, or to taste
3 large red capsicum, quartered, seeded, grilled until
    blackened, peeled and cut into 2cm strips
180g (1 cup) Ligurian olives or other small black olives
1 large ciabatta loaf, sliced and toasted

Wilted chicory and roasted onions
2 spanish onions, unpeeled
½ cup olive oil
1 bunch of chicory (about 750g)

Rinse drained beans well and place in a large saucepan with potato, onion, celery and bay leaf, add 2 litres cold water and bring to the boil. Reduce heat to a low simmer and cook for 1½ hours or until beans are tender. Discard celery and bay leaf, then strain beans, onion and potato over a bowl, reserving cooking liquid. Peel beans, discarding skins.

Process peeled beans, onion, potato and ⅓ cup reserved cooking liquid in a food processor until smooth. With the motor running, gradually add olive oil and process until incorporated, then add lemon juice and process until well combined. Transfer to a bowl, season to taste with sea salt and freshly ground black pepper, then cover and refrigerate for at least 1 hour for flavours to develop, or refrigerate for up to 4 days.

Meanwhile, for wilted chicory and roasted onions,

place onions on a sheet of aluminium foil and drizzle with ¼ cup olive oil to coat. Seal edges of foil to form an airtight package, then place on an oven tray and roast at 200C for 1 hour or until onions are tender when pierced with a knife.

Trim stalks from chicory and discard, then wash and drain well. Heat remaining olive oil in a large frying pan, add chicory and cook over medium heat, tossing until wilted, then season to taste. Transfer wilted chicory to a bowl. Cool onions slightly, then peel and slice into 6 wedges.

To serve, bring dip to room temperature and thin, if necessary, with a little remaining cooking liquid. Serve with wilted chicory, roasted onions, roasted red capsicum, olives and toasted ciabatta to the side.
Serves 8

Olive pastes with lavosh

You can also use these olive pastes in salad dressings, tossed through pasta or served with roasted meats.

Lavosh crispbreads, grissini or crostini, to serve

Black olive paste

160g (1 cup) kalamata olives, pitted

4 anchovy fillets, drained

1 tablespoon drained capers

1 clove of garlic, finely chopped

1½ tablespoons lemon juice

¼ cup extra virgin olive oil

2 teaspoons cognac, or to taste

Green olive and semi-dried tomato paste

160g (1 cup) green olives, pitted

¼ cup drained semi-dried tomatoes

1 clove of garlic, finely chopped

1 tablespoon drained capers

1 tablespoon red wine vinegar

¼ cup olive oil

For black olive paste, process all ingredient except oil and cognac in a food processor until finely chopped. With motor running, gradually add olive oil and process until a smooth paste forms. Stir in cognac and season to taste with freshly ground black pepper.

For green olive and semi-dried tomato paste, process all ingredients except vinegar and oil in a food processor until finely chopped. With motor running, gradually add vinegar and oil and process until smooth. Season to taste with freshly ground black pepper.

Serve with lavosh crispbreads, grissini or crostini.

Makes about ¾ cup black olive paste and about 1 cup green olive and semi-dried tomato paste

Swordfish skewers with chilli-lime dressing

600g swordfish steaks (about 1.5cm thick)
20 small bamboo skewers, soaked in warm water
   for 30 minutes
110g (¾ cup) ground rice
Light olive oil
1 butter lettuce, leaves separated, washed and dried
Chilli-lime dressing
⅓ cup fish sauce
⅓ cup lime juice
2 tablespoons kecap manis
1 clove of garlic, finely chopped
1 fresh long red chilli, seeded and thinly sliced

For chilli-lime dressing, place all ingredients in a bowl and combine well.

Pat fish dry with absorbent paper, then cut into twenty 1.5x8cm strips and thread each strip lengthways onto a skewer. Spread ground rice on a plate, then coat 2 opposite long sides of each piece of fish with ground rice and shake off excess. Heat enough oil in a frying pan to just coat the base and cook fish skewers, in batches, over medium-high heat for 1 minute on each ground rice-coated side or until cooked to your liking. Serve fish skewers immediately with lettuce leaves and drizzled with chilli-lime dressing or with dressing passed separately in a small bowl for dipping.
Makes 20

Chicken empanadas

Purchased puff pastry can be substituted for the home-made pastry.

100g (½ cup) raisins
2 tablespoons dry sherry
400g chicken thigh fillets, trimmed
2 tablespoons tomato paste
Olive oil
1 onion, finely chopped
2 cloves of garlic, finely chopped
70g large green olives (about 10),
    pitted and coarsely chopped
1 egg, lightly beaten with
    1 teaspoon water

Pastry
500g (3⅓ cups) plain flour
125g cold unsalted butter, chopped
1 egg

For pastry, process flour, butter and ½ teaspoon salt in a food processor until mixture resembles breadcrumbs, then add egg and process until just combined. With motor running, add about 200ml iced water or enough to just bring dough together, then form into a disc, wrap with plastic wrap and refrigerate for 20 minutes.

Place raisins in a small bowl, add sherry and set aside. Place chicken and tomato paste in a saucepan and add just enough water to cover. Bring to the boil, reduce heat, then simmer chicken over low heat for 20 minutes or until just cooked through. Remove from heat and stand chicken in liquid until cool.

Meanwhile, heat 2 tablespoons oil in a frying pan, add onion and cook over low-medium heat for 5 minutes or until soft, then add garlic and cook for another minute. Remove from heat and cool.

Drain chicken, reserving cooking liquid, then coarsely chop. Using the pulse button, process chopped chicken, 2 tablespoons reserved cooking liquid, onion mixture, olives, raisins and sherry in a food processor until finely chopped and well combined, taking care not to overprocess. Season to taste with sea salt and freshly ground black pepper.

Roll out dough on a lightly floured surface until 2-3mm thick, then, using a 10cm pastry cutter, cut out rounds from pastry. Place heaped teaspoons of chicken mixture on one side of each pastry round, then moisten pastry edges lightly with water. Fold over pastry to form a semi-circle, then press with fingertips or the back of a fork to seal well. Transfer empanadas to baking paper-lined oven trays, brush lightly with egg mixture, then bake at 190C for 20 minutes or until golden and crisp. Serve immediately.

Makes 25-30

Note: To reheat empanadas, bake at 170C for 10 minutes or until heated through.

Rare beef fillet with crostini and beetroot marmalade

1.6kg fillet of beef, trimmed
⅓ cup olive oil
1 square-shaped loaf of sourdough bread
½ cup horseradish cream
Beetroot marmalade
4 beetroot (about 760g)
1 tablespoon olive oil
1 onion, halved and thinly sliced
2 teaspoons brown mustard seeds
1 teaspoon cumin seeds
55g (¼ cup) caster sugar
⅓ cup apple cider vinegar
1 tablespoon balsamic vinegar
Finely grated rind and juice of 1 orange

Pat beef fillet dry with absorbent paper, then fold tail end of fillet under and, using kitchen string, tie at 5cm intervals to form a compact shape. Brush beef with a little olive oil. Heat a large non-stick frying pan over high heat, add beef and cook, turning frequently, for 3-4 minutes or until browned all over. Transfer beef to a roasting pan, drizzle with 1 tablespoon olive oil, season to taste with freshly ground black pepper and roast at 220C for 25-30 minutes for rare or until cooked to your liking. Remove beef from oven, cover loosely with foil and rest for 15 minutes.

Meanwhile, for beetroot marmalade, peel beetroot and coarsely grate. Heat olive oil in a large saucepan, add onion and cook, stirring occasionally, for 5 minutes or until soft. Add mustard and cumin seeds and cook over medium heat until seeds begin to pop. Add beetroot with sugar, vinegars, orange rind and juice, and ½ cup water, then season to taste with sea salt and freshly ground black pepper. Bring to the boil, reduce heat to low and cook for 45 minutes, stirring frequently, or until mixture is thick. Remove from heat and cool.

Cut bread into 1cm-thick slices, then cut in half. Brush bread with remaining olive oil, then char-grill on both sides until lightly browned.

To serve, thinly slice beef fillet and place on crostini, then top with a small spoonful of horseradish cream and a spoonful of beetroot marmalade.
Serves 24

Rich chocolate cake

250g dark couverture
  chocolate, chopped
⅓ cup buttermilk
250g soft unsalted butter,
  plus extra, for greasing
220g (1 cup) caster sugar
6 eggs, separated
½ teaspoon vanilla extract
125g (1 cup) ground almonds
150g (1 cup) plain flour, sifted
Dutch-process cocoa, for dusting
Blueberries, optional, to serve

Combine chocolate and buttermilk in a small saucepan and stir over very low heat until chocolate melts, then remove from heat and cool.

Using an electric mixer, beat butter and sugar in a large bowl until light and fluffy, then add egg yolks, one at a time, beating well after each. Stir in vanilla and chocolate mixture, then fold in combined ground almonds and flour until just incorporated.

Using an electric mixer, whisk egg whites until stiff peaks form, then, using a large metal spoon, gently fold into chocolate mixture until just combined. Spoon cake mixture into a greased and base-lined 20cm square cake tin and bake at 180C for 40 minutes. Reduce oven temperature to 160C and bake for another 20-25 minutes or until a cake tester withdraws clean. Cool cake in tin for 5 minutes, then turn out onto a wire rack to cool.

Dust cooled cake generously with cocoa and cut into 5cm squares, then serve with blueberries, if using.

Cake will keep in an airtight container for up to 4 days.

Serves 16

Almond grilled figs

24 ripe but firm black or green figs
125ml Amaretto
220g (1 cup) caster sugar
90g (¾ cup) ground almonds
¼ teaspoon ground cinnamon
300g mascarpone, stirred with a wooden
   spoon until thick, to serve

Cut figs in half lengthways and brush cut sides with
liqueur. Combine sugar, almonds and cinnamon in
a shallow bowl. Place figs, cut-side down and one at
a time, in sugar mixture, pressing down gently to coat,
then place, coated-side up, on a baking paper-lined
oven tray. Cook figs under a hot grill for 3-5 minutes or
until sugar is caramelised, then transfer to a large platter
and cool to room temperature. Serve figs topped with
a spoonful of mascarpone, or serve passed separately.
Serves 24

Rose marshmallows

500g granulated sugar
1 tablespoon liquid glucose
2 tablespoons powdered gelatine
2 egg whites
½ teaspoon rosewater, or to taste
Red food colouring, optional
80g (½ cup) icing sugar, sifted
70g (½ cup) cornflour
Dried rose petals, to serve

Combine granulated sugar, glucose and 190ml water in a large heavy-based saucepan and stir over low heat until sugar dissolves. Bring to the boil without stirring and cook until syrup reaches hard-ball stage or 121C on a sugar thermometer.

Meanwhile, sprinkle gelatine over 190ml water in a small heatproof bowl and stand for 10 minutes, then place bowl in a small saucepan of simmering water and stir until gelatine dissolves. Add dissolved gelatine to sugar syrup, taking care as mixture will splutter.

Using an electric mixer, beat egg whites until stiff peaks form, then, with motor running, gradually pour hot syrup down side of the bowl in a thin, steady stream. Add rosewater and a few drops of red food colouring, if using, then whisk until mixture is thick and holds its shape.

Dust a lightly oiled 3cm-deep 20x30cm tin with 2 tablespoons of combined icing sugar and cornflour, then pour marshmallow mixture into tin, smooth top and stand for 2 hours.

Dust a work surface with half the remaining icing sugar mixture and turn out set marshmallow. Using a large knife dipped in hot water, cut marshmallow into 2.5cm squares, then toss to coat in remaining sugar mixture. Stand marshmallows for 1 hour to allow surface to dry, then store in an airtight container for up to 1 week. Serve scattered with dried rose petals.
Makes about 35

Steamed crab rice paper rolls

50g rice vermicelli noodles

250g cooked blue swimmer crab meat,
    drained on absorbent paper

150g jicama (yam bean), peeled and
    cut into julienne

2 shallots, finely chopped

¼ cup dried black fungus, soaked
    in hot water for 10 minutes,
    then drained and chopped

4 green onions, chopped

2 egg yolks, lightly beaten

26 18cm rice paper rounds

Dipping sauce

2 tablespoons fish sauce, or to taste

2 tablespoons rice vinegar

1 fresh small red chilli, finely chopped

2 tablespoons caster sugar

3 cloves of garlic, finely chopped

½ carrot, cut into julienne

For dipping sauce, combine all ingredients in a bowl and stir until sugar dissolves.

Place noodles in a bowl, cover with boiling water and stand for 10 minutes or until soft, then drain well. Using kitchen scissors, cut noodles into 5cm lengths.

Combine crabmeat, jicama, shallots, chopped fungus, green onions and drained noodles in a large bowl. Add egg yolks and season to taste with sea salt and freshly ground black pepper.

Soak a sheet of rice paper in hot water for 5-10 seconds or until just soft, then drain on absorbent paper. Place 1 tablespoon crab mixture 2cm from bottom edge of rice paper, leaving 2cm on each side. Fold bottom edge of paper over filling, tuck in sides and roll up firmly. Repeat with remaining rice paper rounds and filling. Place rice paper rolls in a baking paper-lined bamboo steamer, cover and steam, in batches, over boiling water for 4-5 minutes or until heated through. Serve immediately with dipping sauce.
Makes about 26

Barbecued prawns and asparagus with rocket aïoli

36 medium green prawns
   (about 1.4kg), peeled and cleaned,
   leaving tails intact
60ml dry white wine
1 tablespoon thyme, coarsely chopped
Olive oil
Grated rind and juice of 1 lemon
750g asparagus
   (about 3 bunches), trimmed
12 bamboo skewers, soaked in warm
   water for 30 minutes
Lemon wedges, to serve
Rocket aïoli
150g rocket (about 1 bunch), trimmed
2 egg yolks
1 teaspoon wholegrain mustard
1 clove of garlic, finely crushed
⅔ cup light olive oil
¾ cup crème fraîche

For rocket aïoli, add rocket to a small saucepan of boiling water and drain immediately, then refresh in iced water and drain again. Squeeze excess water from rocket, pat dry, then chop finely. Process egg yolks, mustard, garlic and a pinch of sugar in a food processor until combined. With motor running, gradually add oil in a steady stream until thickened, add rocket and process until smooth, then stir in crème fraîche and season to taste with sea salt and freshly ground black pepper. Makes 1¼ cups.

Combine prawns, wine, thyme, 2 tablespoons olive oil, lemon rind and juice, and freshly ground black pepper to taste in a bowl and mix well. Cover and refrigerate for 1 hour.

Brush asparagus lightly with olive oil and barbecue or char-grill, in batches, until lightly charred all over, then season to taste. Drain prawns from marinade and discard marinade. Thread 3 prawns onto each soaked bamboo skewer, brush lightly with olive oil and barbecue or char-grill, in batches, until just cooked through.

Serve prawns with asparagus, rocket aïoli and lemon wedges.

Serves 12

Merguez sausage sandwiches with sweet and sour onions

Olive oil

4 large onions, thinly sliced

½ cup sherry vinegar

2 tablespoons brown sugar

12 merguez sausages or other
spicy sausages

2 loaves turkish bread, split
lengthwise and toasted

4 red capsicum, quartered,
seeded, grilled until
blackened, peeled and
cut into 3cm pieces

Heat 2 tablespoons olive oil in a frying pan, add onions and cook over medium heat for 5 minutes or until just beginning to soften. Add vinegar, cover and cook for another 20 minutes or until onions are very soft. Add sugar and stir for 2 minutes over high heat or until mixture caramelises, then season to taste with sea salt and freshly ground black pepper. Cool.

Place sausages in a saucepan, cover with water and bring to the boil. Drain and cool. Butterfly sausages, then cut in half widthways. Heat 2 teaspoons olive oil in a frying pan and cook, in batches, until browned on both sides.

Divide sweet and sour onions over toasted turkish bread bases, top with grilled capsicum and sausages and replace lids, then cut each loaf into 6 or 8 and secure each sandwich with a piece of kitchen string, if desired.

Serves 12-16

Char-grilled lamb cutlets with ravigote sauce and balsamic mushrooms

16 lamb cutlets (about 1.1kg),
    french trimmed
Olive oil
Crusty bread, to serve
Ravigote sauce
1 tablespoon baby capers, rinsed and
    finely chopped
10 anchovy fillets, drained and chopped
2 cups (firmly packed) flat-leaf parsley
½ cup chervil leaves
⅓ cup finely chopped chives
2 tablespoons tarragon leaves
1 tablespoon finely chopped rosemary
2 egg yolks
½ cup extra virgin olive oil
2 teaspoons tarragon vinegar
Balsamic mushrooms
16 large cup mushrooms,
    stalks trimmed slightly
¼ cup olive oil
1-2 tablespoons aged balsamic vinegar

For ravigote sauce, process capers, anchovies, 1 teaspoon salt, and herbs in a food processor until finely chopped, then add egg yolks and pulse until combined. Transfer to a bowl and stir in oil and vinegar. Season to taste with sea salt and freshly ground black pepper, then cover closely with plastic wrap and refrigerate until required. Makes about 1¼ cups.

Season lamb cutlets to taste, brush lightly with olive oil and char-grill or barbecue, in batches, for 2 minutes on each side for medium rare or until cooked to your liking, then rest in a warm place for 5 minutes.

Meanwhile, for balsamic mushrooms, brush mushrooms with olive oil, season to taste and char-grill or barbecue, in batches, for 1-2 minutes on each side, then transfer to a platter and drizzle with balsamic vinegar. Place lamb cutlets over mushrooms, spoon over a little ravigote sauce, then serve warm or at room temperature with remaining sauce and crusty bread passed separately.

Serves 8

Fattoush

1 cup olive oil

2 pieces lebanese bread, quartered

500g grape tomatoes or small cherry tomatoes, halved

2 lebanese cucumbers, finely chopped

1½ cups flat-leaf parsley, coarsely chopped

1½ cups mint leaves, coarsely chopped

1 red capsicum, finely chopped

4 radishes, halved and thinly sliced

4 green onions, finely chopped

1 tablespoon sumac

½ cup extra virgin olive oil

2 tablespoons lemon juice

Heat olive oil in a large saucepan over medium heat, and, when hot, add half the lebanese bread and fry for 1½ minutes on each side or until golden, then drain on absorbent paper. Repeat with remaining bread.

Combine tomatoes, cucumbers, parsley, mint, capsicum, radishes and green onions in a large bowl and stir to combine. Coarsely break lebanese bread, toss with vegetable mixture, then sprinkle over sumac, drizzle with extra virgin olive oil and lemon juice, and mix gently to combine. Serve immediately.

Serves 8

Seafood brochettes with dill and coriander dressing

350g squid (about 6), cleaned, tentacles discarded

48 long bamboo skewers, soaked in warm water
   for 30 minutes

1kg baby octopus, cleaned, heads discarded, quartered

700g piece of tuna, cut into 1.5cm pieces

12 butterflied sardines (about 300g)

¼ cup olive oil

Dill and coriander dressing

¼ cup extra virgin olive oil

2 cloves of garlic, finely chopped

2 tablespoons lemon juice

1 tablespoon coriander seeds

1 teaspoon wholegrain mustard

1 tablespoon chopped dill

For dill and coriander dressing, combine olive oil, garlic and lemon juice in a bowl. Place coriander seeds in a small frying pan and stir over medium heat for 2-3 minutes or until fragrant. Cool, then crush in a mortar, using a pestle. Add crushed coriander seeds, mustard and dill to dressing, season to taste with sea salt and freshly ground black pepper, and stir to combine.

Cut through squid hoods on one side to open up, then cut into 3 lengthways and thread 1-2 pieces lengthways onto each of 12 soaked skewers. Thread 2-3 pieces of octopus onto each of a further 12 soaked skewers, then thread 4 pieces of tuna onto each of a further 12 soaked skewers. Thread 1 sardine lengthways onto each of the remaining 12 soaked skewers.

Place skewers in a glass or ceramic dish, drizzle with olive oil and season to taste.

Barbecue or char-grill tuna and octopus, in batches, for 2-3 minutes on each side or until just cooked through. Barbecue or char-grill squid and sardines for 1-2 minutes on each side or until just cooked through. Serve seafood brochettes drizzled with dressing.

Makes 48 skewers

Prawn, kipfler potato and watercress salad with lemon mayonnaise

1.2kg kipfler potatoes, scrubbed and halved
600g fresh peas, podded (200g podded peas)
4 lebanese cucumbers, thinly sliced
100g picked watercress sprigs (about 1 bunch)
12 baby cos lettuce leaves
48 small cooked prawns (about 1.5kg), peeled
   and cleaned, leaving tails intact
Lemon mayonnaise
2 eggs
2 tablespoons Dijon mustard
¼ cup lemon juice
⅔ cup light olive oil
2 tablespoons chopped tarragon

Cook potatoes in lightly salted boiling water until tender, then drain well and cool. Cook peas in lightly salted boiling water for 5 minutes or until tender, drain and refresh under cold running water, then drain again.

For lemon mayonnaise, process eggs, mustard and lemon juice in a food processor until just combined, then, with motor running, add oil in a thin steady stream and process until thick and creamy. Transfer lemon mayonnaise to a bowl and season to taste with sea salt and freshly ground black pepper, then stir in tarragon.

Just before serving, cut cooled potatoes on the diagonal into 2-3cm slices, then place in a large bowl with peas, cucumber and watercress sprigs and toss gently to combine. Spoon salad among lettuce leaves, top with prawns, drizzle with lemon mayonnaise and serve immediately.

Serves 12

Pan bagnat

Pan bagnat can be made a day ahead and stored refrigerated until ready to serve.

1 large eggplant (about 500g),
   cut into 2cm-thick slices
½ cup extra virgin olive oil
16 small dinner rolls
4 ripe egg tomatoes, seeded and
   coarsely chopped
3 red capsicum, quartered, seeded,
   grilled until blackened, peeled and
   coarsely chopped
100g pitted kalamata olives
½ small spanish onion, very thinly sliced
1 tablespoon red wine vinegar
170g jar artichoke hearts marinated in oil,
   drained and coarsely chopped
4 hard-boiled eggs, sliced
⅔ cup pesto

Brush eggplant slices on both sides with ¼ cup olive oil, then place on an oven tray and bake at 200C for 15 minutes or until golden and tender, turning once. Cool, then cut each slice into quarters.

Cut the top off each bread roll and reserve, then scoop out some of the bread, leaving a shell about 1cm thick. Combine tomatoes, capsicum, olives, onion and eggplant in a bowl, season to taste with sea salt and freshly ground black pepper, drizzle with red wine vinegar and remaining olive oil, then toss gently to combine.

Divide vegetable mixture among bread rolls, then top with a layer of artichoke and egg slices. Spoon a little pesto over egg slices, then replace bread roll tops and wrap tightly in plastic wrap. Refrigerate for at least 1 hour to allow flavours to develop. Unwrap rolls and serve cut in half.
Makes 32

Potato, radicchio and hazelnuts with parsley salad cream

2kg chat potatoes

½ cup olive oil

1 head of radicchio

125g hazelnuts, roasted, peeled
  and coarsely chopped

2 tablespoons lemon juice

1 tablespoon Dijon mustard

½ teaspoon caster sugar

1 cup flat-leaf parsley, chopped

¼ cup pouring cream

Place potatoes in a large roasting pan, drizzle with ¼ cup olive oil, season to taste with sea salt and freshly ground black pepper, and toss to combine. Roast potatoes at 200C for 50 minutes or until golden and tender, shaking pan occasionally. Remove from oven and cool.

Remove outer leaves from radicchio and discard. Trim base and separate leaves, then wash and pat dry. Tear radicchio leaves into bite-sized pieces and place in a large bowl, add potatoes and hazelnuts and toss gently to combine.

Process remaining olive oil, lemon juice, mustard, sugar and parsley in a food processor until combined. Add cream, season to taste and pulse until just combined. Drizzle potato salad with parsley salad cream and serve immediately.

Serves 8

Bean, pancetta and bocconcini salad

200g (1 cup) dried flageolet beans, soaked
   overnight in cold water and drained
700g baby green beans, trimmed
15 thin slices pancetta
180g cherry bocconcini, thinly sliced
⅓ cup lemon-pressed extra virgin olive oil
1½ tablespoons red wine vinegar
1 tablespoon tarragon mustard

Place drained flageolet beans in a large saucepan, cover with plenty of cold water and bring to the boil, then simmer for 80 minutes or until tender. Drain beans well, then spread out on a tray and cool.

Cook green beans in a large saucepan of boiling salted water for 2-3 minutes, drain and refresh in iced water, then drain again.

Heat a large frying pan over medium-high heat and, when hot, add pancetta in a single layer and cook for 1 minute on each side or until crisp. Drain on absorbent paper, cool, then break into large pieces.

Combine pancetta, bocconcini, flageolet and green beans in a large bowl.

Whisk together olive oil, vinegar and mustard in a small bowl until well combined, season to taste with sea salt and freshly ground black pepper, then drizzle over salad and toss gently to combine. Serve immediately.
Serves 8

Grilled haloumi with lebanese eggplant salad

4 250g packets of haloumi

16 thin bamboo skewers, soaked in warm
   water for 30 minutes

Olive oil

2 cloves of garlic, finely chopped

2 tablespoons finely chopped mint

4 lebanese breads, split, toasted and
   coarsely broken, to serve

Cos lettuce leaves and lemon wedges,
   optional, to serve

Lebanese eggplant salad

12 lebanese eggplant

2 spanish onions, cut into 8 wedges,
   leaving root end intact

6 cloves of garlic, peeled

2 tablespoons pomegranate molasses

1 tablespoon white wine vinegar

1 teaspoon dried mint

Olive oil

8 egg tomatoes, cut into wedges,
   then halved widthways

For lebanese eggplant salad, add eggplant, onions and garlic to a large saucepan of boiling salted water, cover with a plate to submerge vegetables, then cook over medium heat for 12-15 minutes or until eggplant is tender, then drain well. Cool. Separate onions and garlic from eggplant. Remove skin from eggplant, then cut into 3-4cm rounds and place in a bowl. Trim root end from onions and add wedges to eggplant. Finely chop cooked garlic, then place in a bowl with pomegranate molasses, vinegar, mint and ½ cup olive oil, season to taste with sea salt and freshly ground black pepper, and whisk until well combined. Add dressing to eggplant mixture with tomatoes and toss gently to combine.

Pat haloumi dry with absorbent paper, then cut each block into slices. Carefully thread 2 pieces of haloumi onto each skewer and brush well with olive oil. Combine 2 tablespoons olive oil, garlic and chopped mint, then set aside. Char-grill haloumi on a barbecue hot plate or cook in a non-stick frying pan, in batches, for 2 minutes on each side or until browned. Brush haloumi with oil and garlic mixture and serve with eggplant salad, lebanese bread, and cos lettuce leaves and lemon wedges, if using.

Serves 8

Coconut ice-cream with frozen mango

5 ripe mangoes
Coconut ice-cream
200g (2¼ cups) desiccated coconut
1.5 litres milk
240g shaved coconut palm sugar
12 egg yolks
165g (¾ cup) caster sugar
2 cups pouring cream

Peel and cut cheeks from mangoes, then cut each cheek into 3 wedges. Place mango wedges on baking paper-lined trays, cover and freeze until ready to serve.

For coconut ice-cream, combine coconut and milk in a large saucepan and stand for 15 minutes. Stir in coconut sugar and cook, stirring occasionally, over medium heat until almost boiling. Remove from heat and set aside for 5 minutes for flavours to develop.

Using an electric mixer, beat egg yolks and caster sugar until pale and thick, then strain milk mixture onto egg mixture, pressing down on coconut with the back of a spoon to extract all the milk. Transfer to a saucepan and stir continuously over medium heat until mixture thickens enough to coat the back of a wooden spoon. Do not boil. Remove from heat, stir in cream, then cool to room temperature and refrigerate until cold. Freeze mixture in an ice-cream maker according to manufacturer's instructions. (Depending on the capacity of your ice-cream machine this may need to be done in 2 batches.)

Serve scoops of coconut ice-cream in chilled glasses or cups topped with frozen mango wedges. Ice-cream will keep, frozen in an airtight container, for up to 6 days.
Serves 10-12

Hummingbird cake

If the cake is to be outdoors for any length of time, omit the cream cheese and pecan icing and dust the top heavily with icing sugar.

150g (1 cup) plain flour

75g (½ cup) self-raising flour

½ teaspoon bicarbonate of soda

¼ teaspoon ground cardamom

¼ teaspoon ground nutmeg

½ teaspoon ground cinnamon

200g (1 cup, firmly packed) brown sugar

450g can crushed pineapple in syrup

1 teaspoon vanilla extract

45g (½ cup) desiccated coconut

2 large ripe bananas (about 450g), mashed

2 eggs, lightly beaten

180ml (¾ cup) vegetable oil

60g (½ cup) chopped pecans

Soft butter, for greasing

Cream cheese and pecan icing

30g soft unsalted butter

60g cream cheese, softened

½ teaspoon vanilla extract

240g (1½ cups) icing sugar mixture, sifted

40g (⅓ cup) pecans, roasted and chopped

Sift flours, bicarbonate of soda, spices, sugar and ¼ teaspoon salt into a large bowl. Drain pineapple, pressing with the back of a spoon to extract as much syrup as possible. Reserve ¼ cup of the syrup and add with pineapple to flour mixture. Add vanilla extract, coconut and bananas, and stir with a wooden spoon until well combined. Add eggs and oil and stir until well combined, then fold in chopped pecans. Spoon mixture into a greased and base-lined 20cm round cake tin and bake at 180C for 40 minutes or until a cake tester withdraws clean. Cool cake in tin for 5 minutes before turning out onto a wire rack to cool.

For cream cheese and pecan icing, using an electric mixer, beat butter, cheese and vanilla extract until smooth. With motor running on low speed, gradually add icing sugar mixture and beat until smooth. Spread cooled cake with icing and sprinkle with chopped roasted pecans.

Cake will keep, refrigerated, in an airtight container for 2-3 days.

Serves 10

Strawberries and Pimm's with orange and clove shortbread

1.5kg strawberries, hulled and halved
200ml Pimm's No 1 Cup
75g (⅓ cup) caster sugar
1 cup freshly squeezed and strained
   orange juice
Whipped cream, to serve
Orange and clove shortbread
250g soft unsalted butter
165g (¾ cup) caster sugar
Finely grated rind of 2 oranges
½ teaspoon ground cloves
300g (2 cups) plain flour
100g fine polenta
Cloves, optional, for decoration

For orange and clove shortbread, using an electric mixer, beat butter, sugar and orange rind until light and fluffy, then stir in combined sifted cloves, flour and polenta. Form dough into a disc, wrap in plastic wrap and refrigerate for 1 hour or until firm. Roll out dough on a well-floured surface until 8mm-thick, then, using a 6cm pastry cutter, cut out rounds and place on baking paper-lined oven trays. Press a whole clove into each shortbread, if using, then refrigerate for 1 hour or until firm. Bake shortbread at 160C for 30 minutes or until pale golden and firm to the touch. Cool on trays for 5 minutes, then transfer to a wire rack to cool completely. Shortbread will keep in an airtight container for up to 1 week.

Place strawberries in a bowl, add Pimm's, sugar and orange juice and stir until sugar dissolves, then cover and stand at room temperature for 30 minutes.

Divide strawberries among 12 glasses and serve topped with a little whipped cream, with orange and clove shortbread passed separately, removing whole clove before eating.

Serves 12

Veal with tuna and chive mayonnaise

Olive oil

600g fillet of veal

Pan-fried capers, to serve

Tuna and chive mayonnaise

2 egg yolks

1 teaspoon Dijon mustard

225ml olive oil

95g can tuna in olive oil, drained

1-2 tablespoons lemon juice, to taste

⅓ cup finely chopped chives

Heat a little olive oil in a flameproof dish and cook veal, turning, over high heat until well browned. Transfer to a 200C oven and cook for 25-30 minutes, or until veal is medium rare, then cool.

Meanwhile for tuna and chive mayonnaise, process egg yolks and mustard in a food processor until combined, then, with motor running, gradually add olive oil, drop by drop at first, then in a slow steady steam until mixture is thick and glossy. Add tuna and lemon juice, to taste, and process until smooth. Season to taste with sea salt and freshly ground black pepper and stir in chives and 2 tablespoons water to thin to a drizzling consistency.

Cut veal into thin slices and place, overlapping, in a large shallow bowl or on a platter, spoon tuna and chive mayonnaise over and sprinkle with fried capers.

Serves 8

Oysters with three accompaniments

2 tablespoons olive oil

4 chorizo sausages (about 740g),
   cut into 6mm-thick slices

8 dozen freshly shucked assorted species of oysters

400g ocean trout roe

4 lemons, cut into wedges

Tomato and chive vinaigrette

1½ tablespoons aged red wine vinegar

2 teaspoons lemon juice, or to taste

100ml extra virgin olive oil

2 small shallots, very finely chopped

2 large egg tomatoes, peeled, seeded and finely chopped

½ cup finely chopped chives (about 1 bunch)

For tomato and chive vinaigrette, place vinegar, lemon juice and olive oil in a small bowl and whisk until well combined. Add remaining ingredients, season to taste with sea salt and freshly ground black pepper and stir well. Cover and refrigerate until required.

Heat olive oil in a heavy-based frying pan and cook chorizo slices, in batches, over medium heat for 2-3 minutes on each side or until browned, then drain on absorbent paper.

Place oysters on a large platter and serve with a bowl each of ocean trout roe, warm chorizo, tomato and chive vinaigrette and lemon wedges.

Serves 8-10

Pickled ocean trout with egg mayonnaise

This recipe can be halved if you do not wish to make such a large quantity.

3kg ocean trout, filleted,
  skinned and pin-boned
3 cups cider vinegar
1 tablespoon white peppercorns
1 tablespoon coriander seeds
1½ teaspoons fennel seeds
2 dried bay leaves
⅓ cup sea salt
110g (½ cup) caster sugar
2 onions, peeled and thinly sliced
Egg mayonnaise
4 egg yolks
2 tablespoons Dijon mustard
¼ cup lemon juice, or to taste
350ml olive oil
8 hard-boiled eggs, peeled and
  coarsely chopped

For egg mayonnaise, process egg yolks, mustard and lemon juice in a food processor until smooth, then, with motor running, gradually add olive oil in a slow, steady stream until mixture is thick and glossy. Season to taste with sea salt, freshly ground black pepper and extra lemon juice, then stir in 2-3 tablespoons hot water to thin slightly. Stir chopped eggs into mayonnaise, transfer to a bowl, cover closely with plastic wrap and refrigerate.

Cut each ocean trout fillet crosswise into 4cm-wide slices. Combine vinegar, spices, bay leaves, salt, sugar and 1.5 litres water in a large saucepan and slowly bring to a simmer, stirring to dissolve sugar and salt. Remove from heat and cool completely.

Layer ocean trout and onion slices in a large, deep glass or ceramic dish, then pour vinegar mixture over. Cover dish tightly with plastic wrap and refrigerate for 36 hours before serving. Drain ocean trout and onions and serve with egg mayonnaise. Ocean trout will keep, covered in pickling liquid, in the refrigerator for up to 10 days.
Serves 15-20 as part of a buffet

Crudités with two dips

Blanched cauliflower florets, raw baby carrots, witlof leaves and scrubbed whole radishes could also be served.

400g green beans, trimmed
4 bunches of asparagus (white or green), bases trimmed
Herbed goat's curd dip and warm anchovy dip, recipes follow, to serve

Blanch beans and asparagus, separately, in lightly salted boiling water until just tender, then remove with a slotted spoon and refresh in iced water. Drain well, then pat dry with absorbent paper.
    Serve with herbed goat's curd dip and warm anchovy dip.
Serves 12-14

Herbed goat's curd dip

260g goat's curd
1 cup crème fraîche
¼ cup lemon juice
2 tablespoons finely chopped chives
2 tablespoons finely chopped dill
1 tablespoon finely chopped tarragon
¼ cup finely chopped flat-leaf parsley

Place all ingredients in a bowl and beat with a wooden spoon until smooth and well combined. Season to taste with sea salt and freshly ground black pepper, then cover and refrigerate for 3 hours before serving with crudités.
Makes about 2⅓ cups

Warm anchovy dip

200ml olive oil
4 cloves of garlic, crushed
200g drained anchovy fillets
20 basil leaves, torn
2 teaspoons lemon juice

Place oil and garlic in a small saucepan and cook over low heat until just warm. Place anchovies and basil in a mortar and, using a pestle, pound until a smooth paste forms, then add anchovy mixture to oil mixture and stir to combine well. Add lemon juice, then transfer to a warm bowl and serve with crudités.
Makes about 1¼ cups

Quail in vine leaves with pomegranate, walnut, herb and olive salad

2 tablespoons pomegranate molasses

1 teaspoon sweet paprika

Olive oil

8 quail (about 160g each), halved lengthways

16 large preserved or prepared fresh vine leaves

Pomegranate, walnut, herb and olive salad

1 pomegranate

1 cup coarsely chopped flat-leaf parsley

½ cup coarsely chopped coriander

¼ cup coarsely chopped basil

80g (½ cup) chopped pitted green olives

60g (½ cup) chopped walnuts, roasted

2 green onions, thinly sliced

1 fresh long green chilli, thinly sliced

2 tablespoons extra virgin olive oil

1 tablespoon lemon juice

Combine pomegranate molasses, paprika, 2 tablespoons olive oil, ¼ teaspoon salt and ¼ teaspoon freshly ground black pepper in a small bowl. Place quail halves in a glass or ceramic dish, then pour marinade over and combine well. Cover and refrigerate for 1 hour.

Meanwhile, for pomegranate, walnut, herb and olive salad, gently crush pomegranate by rolling under the palm of your hand on a bench to loosen the seeds. Place a doubled piece of muslin in a sieve over a bowl and cut fruit in half over the muslin, to catch any juice. Remove ⅓ cup seeds and set aside. Place remaining seeds in the muslin and squeeze to extract juice. Reserve 2 tablespoons of pomegranate juice and use remaining juice for another recipe.

Combine herbs, olives, walnuts, green onions and chilli in a bowl. Combine extra virgin olive oil with reserved pomegranate and lemon juices, season to taste with sea salt and freshly ground black pepper and mix well. Just before serving, pour dressing over salad, toss gently to combine, and scatter with pomegranate seeds.

Place 1 vine leaf flat on a work surface, place a quail half on top, fold sides of vine leaf around quail and brush all over with olive oil. Repeat with remaining vine leaves and quail halves.

Heat a large heavy-based frying pan over medium heat and cook quail, in batches, for 5 minutes on each side or until cooked through. Serve immediately with pomegranate, walnut herb and olive salad.

Serves 8

Baked ham with dried peach relish

1 cup pineapple juice

50g glacé ginger

6-7kg cooked leg of ham

35g (⅓ cup) cloves

2 tablespoons Dijon mustard

200g (1 cup, firmly packed) brown sugar

Mature cheddar and a selection of
   breads and grissini, to serve

Dried peach relish

250g dried peaches, coarsely chopped

100g (½ cup, firmly packed) brown sugar

85g (½ cup) seedless raisins

1 cup white wine vinegar

½ teaspoon ground cardamom

¼ teaspoon ground coriander

¼ teaspoon ground cumin

1 teaspoon finely grated orange rind

For dried peach relish, place peaches in a bowl with 1 litre boiling water and soak for 20-30 minutes, then drain, reserving ½ litre of soaking liquid. Combine soaking liquid, peaches and remaining ingredients, except orange rind, in a large saucepan and stir over low heat until sugar dissolves. Bring to the boil and stir frequently (take care that mixture does not stick to base of pan) for 50-60 minutes or until mixture is thick and pulpy. Remove from heat and stir in orange rind, then spoon into an airtight container. Relish will keep in the refrigerator for up to 2 weeks. Makes about 3 cups.

Process pineapple juice and ginger in a food processor until smooth.

Cut through ham rind in a zigzag pattern about 10cm from shank end, then remove rind from the remainder of ham. Score fat in a diamond pattern at 3cm intervals and stud with cloves. Spread with mustard and sprinkle with brown sugar, pressing sugar gently to form a thin coating. Place ham in a large roasting pan and pour 1 cup of water around ham, then bake at 150C for 30 minutes. Baste ham with ginger mixture and bake for another 1 hour, basting with ginger mixture every 20 minutes or until ham is a rich brown colour. Rest ham for 30 minutes before transferring to a platter.

Serve baked ham with dried peach relish, mature cheddar and a selection of breads and grissini.

Serves 30

Note: Tomato chutney and redcurrant jelly can be served as an alternative to the dried peach relish.

Chicken terrine with roast parsnip salad

600g chicken breast fillets, trimmed

350g chicken thigh fillets, trimmed

300g minced chicken

1 tablespoon sea salt, or to taste

¼ teaspoon grated nutmeg

1½ tablespoons finely chopped marjoram

35g (¼ cup) pistachios

7 slices of middle-cut bacon, rind removed

Olive oil, for greasing

Mustard fruits, to serve

Roast parsnip salad

1.2kg small parsnips

⅓ cup extra virgin olive oil

2 bunches of rocket, trimmed

1 avocado, halved, stone, peeled and sliced

2½ tablespoons balsamic vinegar, or to taste

Cut breast and thigh fillets into 1cm pieces, then combine in a large bowl with minced chicken, salt, nutmeg, marjoram, pistachios and freshly ground black pepper to taste, and mix until well combined.

Place slices of bacon across base and up long sides of an oiled 1-litre-capacity loaf tin, making sure there are no gaps and alternating wide pieces with narrow pieces to cover evenly (some slices will hang over the edge). Place a bacon slice over each short end of tin, using trimmed pieces if necessary, then, using your hands, pack chicken mixture into bacon-lined tin and smooth top. Bring overhanging pieces of bacon up over top of terrine, trim any excess and use these pieces to patch gaps. Cover terrine tightly with lightly oiled foil and bake at 180C for 1 hour or until juices run clear when tested with a skewer. Cool terrine to room temperature, then refrigerate for 3 hours or overnight.

For roast parsnip salad, peel parsnips, trim ends and cut into quarters lengthways. Place in a roasting pan, toss in olive oil and roast at 180C for 35 minutes or until tender and lightly browned. Cool slightly, then toss gently in a large bowl with rocket, avocado and balsamic vinegar, and season to taste with sea salt and freshly ground black pepper.

Serve slices of chicken terrine with roast parsnip salad with mustard fruits to the side.

Serves 10

Lobster, prawns and bugs with cauliflower cream and marinated celery

4 small cooked lobster tails (about 300g each),
    halved lengthways and digestive tracts removed
1kg cooked medium prawns, peeled and cleaned,
    leaving tails intact
1kg cooked Balmain or Moreton Bay bugs,
    halved lengthways and digestive tracts removed

Cauliflower cream

25g unsalted butter
450g cauliflower (about ½ cauliflower),
    trimmed and cut into small florets
⅔ cup chicken stock
½ cup pouring cream
2 tablespoons chopped dill

Marinated celery

½ bunch of celery (about 700g)
100ml extra virgin olive oil
1 spanish onion, finely chopped
310ml chardonnay
2½ tablespoons lemon juice
1 tablespoon honey
2 tablespoons drained capers

For cauliflower cream, heat butter in a large saucepan, add cauliflower, stir to coat in butter, then cook, covered, over low heat, stirring occasionally, for 20 minutes or until cauliflower is soft. Add stock, bring mixture to the boil, then cook, covered, for another 5 minutes or until cauliflower is very soft. Remove from heat and cool, then process in a food processor until smooth. Stir cream and dill into purée, season to taste with sea salt and freshly ground black pepper, then cover and refrigerate.

For marinated celery, trim celery, reserving pale green leaves from the heart, peel outer stalks to remove strings, then slice celery thinly. Heat olive oil in a large saucepan, add onion and stir over medium heat for 3 minutes or until soft. Add celery and stir for 3 minutes or until celery just begins to soften. Add remaining ingredients and bring mixture to a simmer. Using a slotted spoon, remove celery from liquid and transfer to a bowl, then boil liquid for 5 minutes or until reduced by one-third. Pour reduced liquid over celery and stand until cool. Coarsely chop reserved celery leaves and stir into mixture, then season to taste.

Place shellfish on a large platter and serve with cauliflower cream and marinated celery.

Serves 8

Whole Atlantic salmon in a salt crust with lemon and spinach orzo

1.5kg sea salt

Soft butter, for greasing

2.5kg whole Atlantic salmon

Herb dressing

1 cup olive oil

¼ cup lemon juice

2 tablespoons each chopped mint,
  coriander and flat-leaf parsley

Lemon and spinach orzo

350g orzo (risoni)

Olive oil

500g spinach (about 1 bunch), trimmed and washed

⅓ cup chopped dill

4 green onions, finely chopped

½ baby cos, trimmed and shredded

¾ cup chopped flat-leaf parsley

Grated rind and juice of 1 lemon

For herb dressing, combine all ingredients and season to taste with sea salt and freshly ground black pepper.

Place a thin layer of salt over a foil-lined oven tray, then place salmon over and pack remaining salt tightly over salmon to completely cover. Roast at 200C for 45 minutes. Remove from oven and rest for 10 minutes before cracking salt crust and removing skin.

Meanwhile, for lemon and spinach orzo, cook orzo in plenty of boiling salted water for 10 minutes or until al dente. Drain, place in a large bowl and toss with ¼ cup olive oil. Heat 2 tablespoons olive oil in a large heavy-based frying pan, add spinach and toss over high heat until wilted, then drain. Coarsely chop spinach and add to pasta with remaining ingredients, season to taste and mix well.

Serve salmon on a bed of lemon and spinach orzo and drizzled with herb dressing.

Serves 8

Couscous, bean and zucchini salad

300g green beans, trimmed and cut into 2cm pieces

2 carrots, cut into 1cm pieces

3 zucchini, trimmed and cut into 1cm pieces

1 litre vegetable stock

120g butter, chopped

600g (3 cups) instant couscous

½ cup mint leaves, coarsely chopped

½ cup coriander leaves, coarsely chopped

150g (1 cup) pistachios, coarsely chopped

Dressing

1 cup Greek-style yoghurt

¼ cup lemon juice

½ cup light olive oil

1½ teaspoons ground cumin

2 teaspoons honey

For dressing, whisk all ingredients until well combined, then season to taste with sea salt and freshly ground black pepper. Cover and refrigerate until required.

Cook beans, carrots and zucchini, separately, in boiling salted water for 1 minute or until just tender, then drain, refresh in iced water and drain again.

Place stock in a saucepan and bring to the boil, add butter and salt to taste and stir until melted, then pour over couscous in a heatproof bowl, cover and stand for 5-6 minutes or until stock has been absorbed. Using a fork, stir to fluff grains, then add blanched vegetables and herbs and toss gently to combine. Transfer mixture to a large bowl, drizzle with dressing and scatter with pistachios.

Serves 12

Beef and olive wellingtons

2 1.5kg fillets of beef, trimmed
320g (2 cups) kalamata olives, pitted
3 anchovy fillets
45g (¼ cup) salted capers, soaked in water, drained
4 green onions, chopped
½ cup flat-leaf parsley leaves
20g rinsed and drained preserved lemon rind
Olive oil
2 375g blocks frozen puff pastry, thawed
2 eggs, lightly beaten
Steamed green beans, to serve

Pat beef fillets dry with absorbent paper, then fold tail end of each fillet under and, using kitchen string, tie at 5cm intervals to form a compact shape.

Process olives, anchovies, drained capers, green onions, parsley, preserved lemon and 2 tablespoons olive oil until a smooth paste forms. Heat 1 tablespoon olive oil in a large frying pan. Add 1 beef fillet to the pan and cook over high heat, turning occasionally, for 4 minutes or until browned all over. Remove and cool completely, then repeat with remaining beef fillet and another tablespoon oil, if necessary.

Roll out 1 packet of puff pastry on a lightly floured surface until 30x45cm, then place pastry onto a large baking paper-lined oven tray. Place a beef fillet in the middle lengthways and spread half the olive paste over fillet, then roll up pastry to enclose fillet and place seam-side down, tucking ends under. Repeat with remaining pastry, fillet and olive paste. Using a sharp knife, cut 2.5cm-long slits in the top of pastry at 5cm intervals along the length and brush with beaten eggs.

Cook beef and olive wellingtons at 180C for 40 minutes or until golden. Remove and rest for 10 minutes before cutting into slices with a serrated knife. Serve immediately with steamed green beans.
Serves 16

Chickpea salad

400g (2 cups) dried chickpeas,
    soaked overnight in cold water
1 cup chopped flat-leaf parsley
6 egg tomatoes, halved, seeded
    and cut into 1.5cm pieces
150g (1½ cups) Ligurian olives,
    or other small black olives
150g rocket leaves
4 hard-boiled eggs, quartered
Dressing
2 tablespoons red wine vinegar
100ml extra virgin olive oil
1 clove of garlic, finely chopped

Drain chickpeas, then place in a large saucepan, cover with cold water and bring to the boil over medium heat. Reduce heat to low and simmer chickpeas for 40 minutes or until tender, then drain well and transfer to a large bowl.

Meanwhile, for dressing, whisk together vinegar, oil and garlic in a small bowl, then season to taste with sea salt and freshly ground black pepper. Pour dressing over warm chickpeas, combine well, then set aside to cool. Add parsley, tomatoes and olives to chickpea mixture and toss to combine, then transfer to a large bowl and mix through rocket leaves and hard-boiled eggs.
Serves 12-16

Lime citron chiffon cake

6 eggs at room temperature, separated
330g (1½ cups) caster sugar
½ cup canola oil
Finely grated rind of 1 lime
½ teaspoon cream of tartar
300g (2 cups) self-raising flour, sifted 3 times
Thinly peeled slices of glacé citron, to decorate
Lime glaze
¼ cup strained freshly squeezed orange juice
1 tablespoon strained freshly squeezed lime juice
350g pure icing sugar, sifted

Using an electric mixer, whisk egg yolks and half the sugar until very thick and pale. With motor on low speed, gradually add canola oil combined with ¾ cup water and whisk until just combined. Stir in lime rind, then transfer to a large bowl.

Using an electric mixer, whisk egg whites until foamy, add cream of tartar and beat until soft peaks form. Gradually add remaining caster sugar and whisk until mixture is thick and glossy.

Add flour to egg yolk mixture and, using a whisk, whisk until just combined, then using a large metal spoon, fold in egg white mixture in 2 batches. Spoon mixture into an ungreased 25cm tube (angel food) cake tin and bake at 170C for 45-50 minutes or until a cake tester withdraws clean. Immediately invert cake tin over the top of a funnel and rest cake in tin until cooled. (This process stops the cake from sinking and retains all the trapped air, creating a light-textured cake.)

For lime glaze, stir juices into icing sugar until mixture is the consistency of pouring cream, adding a little more juice if necessary.

Carefully run a small knife around outer edge of cake tin, then turn cake out onto a wire rack over a tray. Pour glaze over top of cake, allowing mixture to drip down side, then stand until glaze sets.

Serve cake topped with twists of glacé citron.

Serves 8-10

Almond, white chocolate and raspberry cakes

This mixture can easily be doubled to make 24.

60g (½ cup) ground almonds
125g self-raising flour
125g soft unsalted butter
100g caster sugar
2 eggs
60ml Amaretto
75g white couverture chocolate,
   chopped into 3mm pieces
300ml mascarpone
1 tablespoon icing sugar, sifted,
   plus extra, optional, to serve
300g raspberries

Place paper cases into holes of a 12-hole (⅓ cup-capacity) muffin tin. Sift together ground almonds, flour and a pinch of salt.

Using an electric mixer, beat butter and sugar until light and fluffy, add eggs one at a time, beating well after each, then add 2 tablespoons liqueur and beat until just combined. Stir in flour mixture, then stir in white chocolate until just combined. Spoon mixture into paper cases and bake at 190C for 18-20 minutes or until golden and a cake tester withdraws clean. Transfer to a wire rack to cool. Using a small serrated knife, level peaks of cakes, discarding scraps.

Combine mascarpone, icing sugar and remaining liqueur in a small bowl and, using a wooden spoon, stir until thick. Using a small spoon, place spoonfuls of mascarpone mixture on tops of cakes, then divide raspberries among tops, pressing gently into mascarpone mixture. Serve cakes dusted with icing sugar, if using.

Undecorated cakes can be made a day ahead and stored in an airtight container. Decorated cakes are best served on day of making.
Makes 12

Brie en croûte with caramelised apples

Muscatels, toasted walnuts, quince paste or dried fruit are also delicious accompaniments to the brie en croûte.

375g block frozen puff pastry, thawed
1.2kg wheel of ripe brie or camembert
1 egg yolk, lightly beaten with 2 tablespoons water
Caramelised apples
1kg granny smith apples (about 5-6)
Juice of 1 orange
60g unsalted butter, chopped
2 tablespoons caster sugar
¼ teaspoon ground cinnamon

Roll out pastry on a lightly floured surface until 3mm-thick, then trim to a 50cm circle. Place cheese in centre of pastry, gather pastry edges together and bring pastry up and over cheese to cover completely, then secure gathered pastry with kitchen string and trim any excess pastry with scissors. Place cheese on a baking paper-lined oven tray, cover with plastic wrap and refrigerate for at least 1 hour. Brush top of pastry with egg yolk mixture and bake cheese at 200C for 35-40 minutes or until pastry is puffed and golden.

Stand brie en croûte for 20-30 minutes, then remove string.

Meanwhile for caramelised apples, peel, core and slice apples into wedges, then place wedges with orange juice in a large bowl and toss to combine. Remove apple wedges and pat dry with absorbent paper. Melt half the butter in a large frying pan, add half the apple wedges in a single layer and cook over medium heat until golden, then turn and sprinkle with 1 tablespoon sugar and a pinch of cinnamon. Cook for 3-4 minutes on each side or until apples are tender, then remove from pan. Repeat with remaining butter, apples, sugar and cinnamon.

Serve brie en croûte warm or at room temperature, cut into wedges, with caramelised apples to the side.
Serves 14-16

Merlot-poached fruits with basil and cream

2 750ml bottles merlot
440g (2 cups) caster sugar
2 sticks of cinnamon
3 star anise
1 vanilla bean, split lengthways
10 firm corella or packham pears
8 small green apples
8 tamarillos
1 cup basil leaves
Double cream, to serve

Combine red wine, sugar, cinnamon, star anise, scraped seeds of vanilla bean and bean with 750ml water in a large saucepan and bring to the boil over high heat. Reduce heat to medium and simmer for 5 minutes.

Peel and halve pears, then, using a melon baller, remove cores. Add pears to poaching liquid and simmer very gently, so that bubbles are barely breaking the surface of cooking liquid, for 10 minutes. Peel and halve apples, then, using a melon baller, remove cores and cut in half again, then add to the liquid. Cover fruits with a circle of baking paper and simmer very gently for 25 minutes. Halve tamarillos and add to the poaching liquid, re-cover with baking paper and cook for another 10-15 minutes or until tamarillos are very soft but intact. Remove pan from heat, add basil and stir gently, then cool fruits in syrup. Remove skins from cooled tamarillos. Serve fruits with a little cooking syrup and a spoonful of double cream, passed separately.
Serves 12

Strawberry apple slush

250g strawberries, hulled
1 cup apple juice
Juice of 1 lime
1 tablespoon caster sugar, or to taste
1 cup crushed ice
Chilled soda water, optional, to serve

Process strawberries, juices, sugar and crushed ice
in a blender until mixture is finely chopped and 'slushy'.
Divide between highball glasses, top with soda water,
if using, and serve immediately.
Serves 4-6

Gin mint julep

6 mint leaves
1¼ teaspoons caster sugar, or to taste
1 teaspoon lime juice
50ml gin
Crushed ice and cocktail swizzle stick, optional, to serve

Place mint, sugar and lime juice in a highball glass, then,
using a wooden spoon or end of a rolling pin, pound
until coarsely crushed. Pour in gin and fill glass with
crushed ice, then serve with a cocktail swizzle stick
to stir, if using.
Serves 1

Raspberry and prosecco fizz

240g raspberries
175g caster sugar
1 tablespoon lemon juice
2 tablespoons crème de cassis
2 750ml bottles prosecco (Italian sparkling wine), chilled

Divide half the raspberries among ice cube trays, placing 2 raspberries in each hole, then fill with enough water to cover raspberries and freeze for 4 hours or until frozen.

Combine sugar, lemon juice and ¼ cup boiling water in a saucepan and stir until well combined. Add remaining raspberries and stir over low heat until sugar dissolves, then simmer gently for 10 minutes. Strain through a fine sieve (do not press down on berries) for about 15 minutes. Cool, then stir in crème de cassis. Raspberry syrup will keep refrigerated for up to 1 week. Makes about 175ml syrup.

To serve, place a raspberry ice cube in the base of each wine glass or champagne flute, add 1 tablespoon raspberry syrup, then fill glasses with prosecco and serve immediately.

Serves 16

Fresh tomato, basil and oyster shooters

Ice
100ml vodka
¼ cup finely chopped basil
2 large vine-ripened tomatoes, peeled,
    seeded and chopped
¼ small red capsicum, peeled and chopped
1 tablespoon finely chopped spanish onion
2 tablespoons lemon juice
½ teaspoon worcestershire sauce
Tabasco sauce, to taste
16 freshly shucked oysters
1 green onion, very thinly sliced

Fill a cocktail shaker two-thirds full with ice, add vodka and basil and shake vigorously, then, using a fine sieve, strain into a bowl.

Blend tomatoes, capsicum, onion, lemon juice, worcestershire sauce, Tabasco, ¼ teaspoon sea salt and 10 ice cubes in a blender until smooth. Add vodka mixture and process until just combined, then divide among sixteen 40ml-capacity shot glasses. Top each glass with an oyster, a little green onion and freshly ground black pepper.

Makes 16 shooters

Orange wine

This drink needs to be made 3 days before using, but once made will last indefinitely.

220g (1 cup) caster sugar
750ml dry white wine
250ml brandy
Finely grated rind of 4 oranges
Chilled sparkling mineral water, optional, to taste

Combine sugar and ½ cup water in a saucepan, slowly bring to the boil, stirring occasionally to dissolve sugar, then remove from heat and cool. Combine syrup with wine, brandy and orange rind in a large jug, then pour into sterilised bottles, seal and refrigerate for 3 days to allow flavours to develop.

Strain wine through a muslin-lined sieve, return to bottles and seal. Orange wine will keep in the refrigerator indefinitely. Serve wine chilled, topped with sparkling mineral water to taste, if using.
Makes about 1.25 litres

Wine punch

110g (½ cup) caster sugar
2 sticks of cinnamon
½ cup freshly squeezed orange juice
½ cup freshly squeezed lime juice
750ml light-bodied red wine, chilled
175ml Bacardi rum
1 orange, halved and thinly sliced
1 lime, halved and thinly sliced
200ml sparkling mineral water, chilled

Combine sugar, cinnamon and ¼ cup water in a small saucepan and slowly bring to a simmer, stirring until sugar dissolves. Remove from heat, transfer syrup mixture to a large bowl and cool. Stir orange and lime juices, red wine, Bacardi and sliced orange and lime into syrup mixture, then pour into a large jug and chill thoroughly. Just before serving, add mineral water and serve in tall glasses as an aperitif.
Serves 6

AMARETTO: almond-flavoured liqueur from Italy.

AVRUGA: a black fish roe from the golden herring, imported from Spain. Available from specialty food stores.

BAKING POWDER: a raising agent that is two parts cream of tartar to one part bicarbonate of soda (baking soda).

BALMAIN (OR MORETON BAY) BUG: a crustacean with white flesh and a rich sweet flavour. Substitute crayfish or prawns.

BEETROOT: beets or red beets.

BETEL LEAVES: thick, glossy, green heart-shaped leaves with raised veins used as wrappers in Thai cooking; the whole leaf is edible. Available from Asian greengrocers. Substitute with small spinach leaves.

BICARBONATE OF SODA: also known as baking soda.

BUTTER: use salted or unsalted (sweet) butter as directed (125g is equal to one stick of butter).

CAPSICUM: also known as pepper or bell pepper. Discard seeds and membranes.

CASTER SUGAR: superfine or finely granulated table sugar.

CHICORY: a bitter vegetable with slender pale green stems and long dark leaves. Remove most of the tough stems before cooking. Substitute with silverbeet (swiss chard).

CORIANDER: also known as cilantro or chinese parsley.

CORNFLOUR: also known as cornstarch; used as a thickening agent in cooking.

CORNICHONS: tiny sour French gherkins.

COCONUT PALM SUGAR: available from Asian food stores.

COUVERTURE CHOCOLATE: top-quality dark or milk chocolate with a high percentage (50 to 99 per cent) of cocoa butter and cocoa liquor (known as cocoa solids). The higher the cocoa content, the more intense and bitter the chocolate flavour. Sold in large 1-5kg blocks from specialty food stores, it is also available from some delicatessens repackaged in smaller weights.

CREME DE CASSIS: a blackcurrant-flavoured liqueur.

CREME FRAICHE: cultured thick cream with a fresh sour taste. Does not separate when boiled.

CUT INTO JULIENNE: fruits, vegetables or citrus rinds cut approximately 3mm thick in 25mm strips.

DRIED BLACK FUNGUS: available from Asian food stores.

DRIED ROSE PETALS: used in Middle Eastern cooking, specifically Iranian. Available from Middle Eastern food stores.

DUTCH-PROCESS COCOA: 'dutching' is a method of alkalising cocoa. An alkali is added during processing, neutralising the astringent quality of the cocoa and giving it a rich dark colour and smoother, more rounded flavour. Available from specialty food stores and delicatessens.

EGGPLANT: aubergine.

FRENCH-TRIMMED: bone ends cleaned of meat.

GALANGAL: a rhizome resembling ginger in shape but with a pink-hued skin. The flesh is more dense and fibrous than ginger, while the flavour more delicate. Available from Asian greengrocers.

GLACE CITRON: made from a citrus fruit resembling a large rough-skinned lemon. Available from delicatessens and specialty food stores.

GOAT'S CURD: a fresh tangy cheese made from goat's milk. Substitute with crème fraîche.

GRAPE TOMATOES: the shape and size of grapes. Substitute with cherry tomatoes.

GREEN ONION: sometimes called shallot or scallion, an immature onion pulled when the top is still green and before the bulb has formed.

GROUND RICE: available from Asian food stores; substitute rice flour.

HALOUMI: a firm, slightly salty stretched-curd Cypriot cheese made from sheep's milk. Available from some supermarkets and Middle Eastern food stores.

ICING SUGAR: also known as powdered sugar or confectioner's sugar.

JICAMA: yam bean; available from Asian food stores.

KECAP MANIS: a dark sweet soy sauce. Used mostly in Indonesian and Malaysian cooking, the flavour derives from palm sugar and star anise. Available from Asian food stores.

LEBANESE CUCUMBERS: short, thin-skinned and slender; also known as the european or burpless cucumber.

LIQUID GLUCOSE: used in baking and confectionery making as a sweetener, as it does not crystallise easily. Available from health food stores.

MASCARPONE: a fresh, unripened, smooth, triple cream cheese with a rich, sweet slightly acidic taste.

MUSHROOM
Shiitake: also known as chinese black, forest or golden oak; large and meaty with an earthy taste.
Swiss brown: full-flavoured, also known as roman or cremini. Substitute button or cap variety.

MUSTARD FRUITS: *mostarda di frutta* are traditional Italian condiments for boiled meats of which many regional variations exist. Whole or sliced fruits used include orange, apple, pear and quince; the fruit is candied in a syrup flavoured with mustard and spices.

ORZO: tiny rice-shaped pasta; also known as risoni.

POLENTA: yellow or white coarse granular meal made from maize or corn; also called cornmeal.

POTATOES
Chat: baby new potatoes.
Sebago: brown-skinned white-fleshed potato. Suitable for boiling, baking, frying and particularly good for mashing.
Spunta: brown-skinned yellow-fleshed potato. Suitable for baking, frying, mashing and roasting, but not boiling.

PEKING DUCK PANCAKES: available from Asian food stores.

POMEGRANATE MOLASSES: made from the juice of pomegranate seeds boiled down to a thick syrup. Available from Middle Eastern food stores and delicatessens.

PRESERVED LEMONS: lemons preserved in salt and lemon juice. A common ingredient in North African cooking, available from specialty food stores.

PROSECCO: sparkling wine from Italy.

READY-SOAKED FIGS: dried figs that have already been soaked in water, are plump and more moist than regular dried figs. If unavailable, soak dried figs in hot water for 20 minutes or until plump, then drain.

SAFFRON THREADS: the dried stigmas of the crocus flower. Available from specialty food stores and some supermarkets.

SHALLOTS: also known as eschalots or french shallots. Small golden brown bulbs, grown in clusters.

SPANISH ONION: a purplish red onion with a mild flavour. Also known as red onion.

VINE LEAVES: available from delicatessens and some supermarkets.

WASHED-RIND CHEESE: first surface-ripened by bacteria, then washed, it has an orange or white rind and a strong smell.

ZUCCHINI: courgette.

measures

One Australian metric measuring cup holds approximately 250ml, one Australian metric tablespoon holds 20ml, one Australian metric teaspoon holds 5ml. The difference between one country's measuring cups and another's is within a two- or three-teaspoon variance. North America, New Zealand and the United Kingdom use a 15ml tablespoon.

All cup and spoon measurements are level.

We use large eggs with an average weight of 60g.

Unless specified, all fruit and vegetables are medium sized and herbs are fresh.

DRY MEASURES

metric	imperial
15g	½oz
30g	1oz
60g	2oz
90g	3oz
125g	4oz (¼lb)
155g	5oz
185g	6oz
220g	7oz
250g	8oz (½lb)
280g	9oz
315g	10oz
345g	11oz
375g	12oz (¾lb)
410g	13oz
440g	14oz
470g	15oz
500g	16oz (1lb)
750g	24oz (1½lb)
1kg	32oz (2lb)

LIQUID MEASURES

metric	imperial
30ml	1 fluid oz
60ml	2 fluid oz
100ml	3 fluid oz
125ml	4 fluid oz
150ml	5 fluid oz (¼ pint/1 gill)
190ml	6 fluid oz
250ml	8 fluid oz
300ml	10 fluid oz (½ pint)
500ml	16 fluid oz
600ml	20 fluid oz (1 pint)
1000ml (1 litre)	1¾ pints

LENGTH MEASURES

metric	imperial
3mm	⅛in
6mm	¼in
1cm	½in
2cm	¾in
2.5cm	1in
5cm	2in
6cm	2½in
8cm	3in
10cm	4in
13cm	5in
15cm	6in
18cm	7in
20cm	8in
23cm	9in
25cm	10in
28cm	11in
30cm	12in (1ft)

OVEN TEMPERATURES

These oven temperatures are only a guide. Always check the manufacturer's manual.

	°C (Celsius)	°F (Fahrenheit)	Gas Mark
Very slow	120	250	1
Slow	150	300	2
Moderately slow	160	325	3
Moderate	180-190	350-375	4
Moderately hot	200-210	400-425	5
Hot	220-230	450-475	6
Very hot	240-250	500-525	7